Economics of Undiscovered Oil and Gas in the North Slope of Alaska: Economic Update and Synthesis

By Emil D. Attanasi and Philip A. Freeman

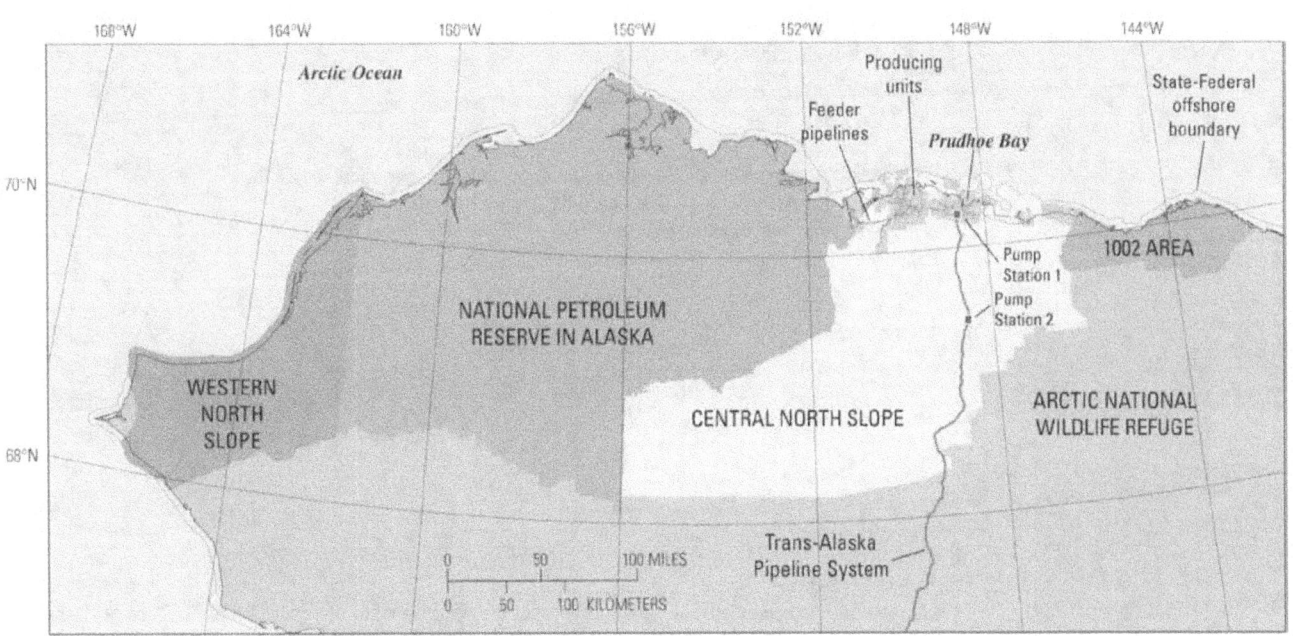

Open-File Report 2009–1112

U.S. Department of the Interior
U.S. Geological Survey

U.S. Department of the Interior
KEN SALAZAR, Secretary

U.S. Geological Survey
Suzette M. Kimball, Acting Director

U.S. Geological Survey, Reston, Virginia: 2009

For product and ordering information:
World Wide Web: http://www.usgs.gov/pubprod
Telephone: 1-888-ASK-USGS

For more information on the USGS—the Federal source for science about the Earth,
its natural and living resources, natural hazards, and the environment:
World Wide Web: http://www.usgs.gov
Telephone: 1-888-ASK-USGS

Suggested citation:
Attanasi, E.D., and Freeman, P.A., 2009, Economics of undiscovered oil and gas in the North Slope of Alaska;
Economic update and synthesis: U.S. Geological Survey Open-File Report 2009–1112, 59 p., available only online.

Cover: Map showing the Alaska North Slope assessment study area, which consists of Federal, Native, and State
lands in the 1002 Area of the Arctic National Wildlife Refuge, the central North Slope, the National Petroleum Reserve
in Alaska (NPRA), and the western North Slope (area west of the NPRA). See figure 1 in text.

Contents

Figures

[List includes figures in appendix 3]

Tables

[List includes tables in appendixes 1, 2, and 3]

Conversion Factors

Inch/Pound to SI

Multiply	By	To obtain
	Length	
foot (ft)	0.3048	meter (m)
mile (mi)	1.609	kilometer (km)
	Area	
acre	4,047	square meter (m^2)
acre	0.4047	hectare (ha)
square mile (640 acres)	2.590	square kilometer
	Volume	
barrel (bbl), (petroleum, 1 barrel=42 gal)	0.1590	cubic meter (m^3)
cubic foot (ft^3)	0.02832	cubic meter (m^3)

Unit Abbreviations

bbl   barrel of crude oil
BBL   billions of barrels of liquids
BBO   billions of barrels of oil
BCF   billions of cubic feet
BOE   barrel of oil equivalent
          = 1 barrel of crude oil
          = 6,000 cubic feet of natural gas
          = 1.5 barrels of natural gas liquids

Btu   British thermal unit
MCF   thousands of cubic feet
MMBO   millions of barrels of oil
TCF   trillions of cubic feet

Economics of Undiscovered Oil and Gas in the North Slope of Alaska: Economic Update and Synthesis

By Emil D. Attanasi and Philip A. Freeman

Abstract

The U.S. Geological Survey (USGS) has published assessments by geologists of undiscovered conventional oil and gas accumulations in the North Slope of Alaska; these assessments contain a set of scientifically based estimates of undiscovered, technically recoverable quantities of oil and gas in discrete oil and gas accumulations that can be produced with conventional recovery technology. The assessments do not incorporate economic factors such as recovery costs and product prices. The assessors considered undiscovered conventional oil and gas resources in four areas of the North Slope: (1) the central North Slope, (2) the National Petroleum Reserve in Alaska (NPRA), (3) the 1002 Area of the Arctic National Wildlife Refuge (ANWR), and (4) the area west of the NPRA, called in this report the "western North Slope." These analyses were prepared at different times with various minimum assessed oil and gas accumulation sizes and with slightly different assumptions. Results of these past studies were recently supplemented with information by the assessment geologists that allowed adjustments for uniform minimum assessed accumulation sizes and a consistent set of assumptions. The effort permitted the statistical aggregation of the assessments of the four areas composing the study area.

At the mean values, 24 billion barrels of oil (BBO) was assessed in 179 oil accumulations and 103 trillion cubic feet (TCF) of undiscovered nonassociated gas was assessed in 145 gas accumulations. The volumes of oil assessed for the NPRA and the 1002 Area of ANWR are about equal and together account for 86 percent of the oil assessed. Nearly all of the remainder of the undiscovered oil was assigned to the central North Slope study subarea. At the mean values, more than 61 percent of the natural gas in gas accumulations was assigned to the NPRA, 24 percent was assigned to the central North Slope subarea, 10 percent was assigned to the western North Slope subarea, and 4 percent was assigned to the 1002 Area of ANWR. For this aggregation, estimates of the 95th and 5th fractiles for oil in undiscovered oil accumulations are 17.4 BBO and 32.4 BBO, respectively, and for undiscovered nonassociated gas (that is, gas in gas accumulations) are 74.3 TCF and 135 TCF, respectively.

The assessment aggregation predicts predominantly modest undiscovered accumulation sizes by North Slope standards. At the 95th fractile, only three accumulations of at least 500 million barrels of oil (MMBO), with total of 2.4 BBO, were predicted. At the mean and 5th-fractile estimates, oil in oil accumulations of at least 500 MMBO amount to about 5.2 BBO (in six accumulations) and 9.3 BBO (in nine accumulations), respectively. Most of these larger oil accumulations were assessed in the 1002 Area of ANWR. Gas accumulations containing at least 3 TCF of gas account for only 4 percent of the assessed nonassociated gas at the 95th-fractile estimates, 12 percent of the gas at the mean estimate, and 19 percent of the gas at the 5th-fractile estimate.

This economic analysis is based on undiscovered assessed accumulation distributions represented by the four-area aggregation and incorporates updates of costs and technological and fiscal assumptions used in the initial economic analysis that accompanied the geologic assessment of each study area. Costs are in constant 2007 dollars. During 2007, refiner acquisition cost for crude oil ranged from $50.77 to $85.29 per barrel. Market prices for natural gas were valued at two-thirds the market prices of energy-equivalent volumes of crude oil, which has been the historical average. Results of the economic analysis are presented as separate cost functions associated with the mean and 95th- and 5th-fractile estimates of technically recoverable oil in oil discoveries and gas in gas discoveries. Because a gas transportation system has not been built, the economic analysis of nonassociated natural gas assumed that there would be either a 10- or a 20-year delay between the expenditures for discovery of gas accumulations and their development and production that would access a gas pipeline to market.

For the entire North Slope study area, at the mean estimate and a market price of $72 per barrel ($8.00 per thousand cubic feet [MCF]), 21.0 BBO and 16.8 TCF of nonassociated gas are predicted to be economic to find, develop, and produce if one assumes constant 2007 costs and technology and the 10-year delay between gas discovery and production for the market. At $72/barrel at the 95th- and 5th-fractile estimates for oil in oil accumulations, the economic oil amounts to 14.5 BBO and 28.8 BBO, respectively. At $8/MCF, the economic nonassociated gas volumes at the 95th- and 5th-fractile estimates for gas in gas accumulations are 10.8 TCF and 31.9 TCF, respectively.

Similarly, at the mean estimate, and a lower market price of $42/barrel ($4.67/MCF), the estimated volume of economically recoverable oil is 14.9 BBO; at the higher price of $108/barrel ($12/MCF), the estimated volume of economic oil is 21.2 BBO. At $4.67/MCF, it is not economic to search for gas accumulations, but at $12/MCF, it is estimated that 62.4 TCF can be found and produced if there is no more than a 10-year delay between discovery and production for a market. Calculations based on the mean of the assessment indicate that the further delay of 10 years added to the initial 10-year delay would reduce the economic nonassociated gas at a market price of $8/MCF to 14.4 TCF from 16.8 TCF and at $12/MCF to 45.3 TCF from 62.4 TCF.

This report is intended to place the geologic resource analysis into an economic context that is informative and easily understood by policymakers and decisionmakers. The scope of the economic analysis is general rather than site or prospect specific. The economic analysis is limited to the evaluation of general finding costs, development costs (including the costs of primary recovery and some aspects of secondary recovery), and the costs of transporting the product to market.

Introduction

The U.S. Geological Survey's assessments of oil and gas in the North Slope of Alaska report a set of scientifically based estimates of undiscovered, technically recoverable quantities of oil and gas in discrete oil and gas accumulations that can be produced with conventional recovery technology. The assessors considered undiscovered conventional oil and gas resources in four areas of the North Slope: (1) the central North Slope (Garrity and others, 2005), (2) the National Petroleum Reserve in Alaska (NPRA) (Bird and Houseknecht, 2002), (3) the 1002 Area of the Arctic National Wildlife Refuge (ANWR) (Bird, 1999), and (4) the area west of the NPRA, called in this report the "western North Slope" (see fig. 1). These analyses were prepared at different times with various minimum assessed oil and gas accumulation sizes and with slightly different assumptions. Results of these past studies were recently supplemented with information by the assessment geologists that allowed adjustments for uniform minimum assessed accumulation sizes and a consistent set of assumptions (appendix 1). The effort permitted the statistical aggregation of the assessments of the four areas composing the study area shown in figure 1.

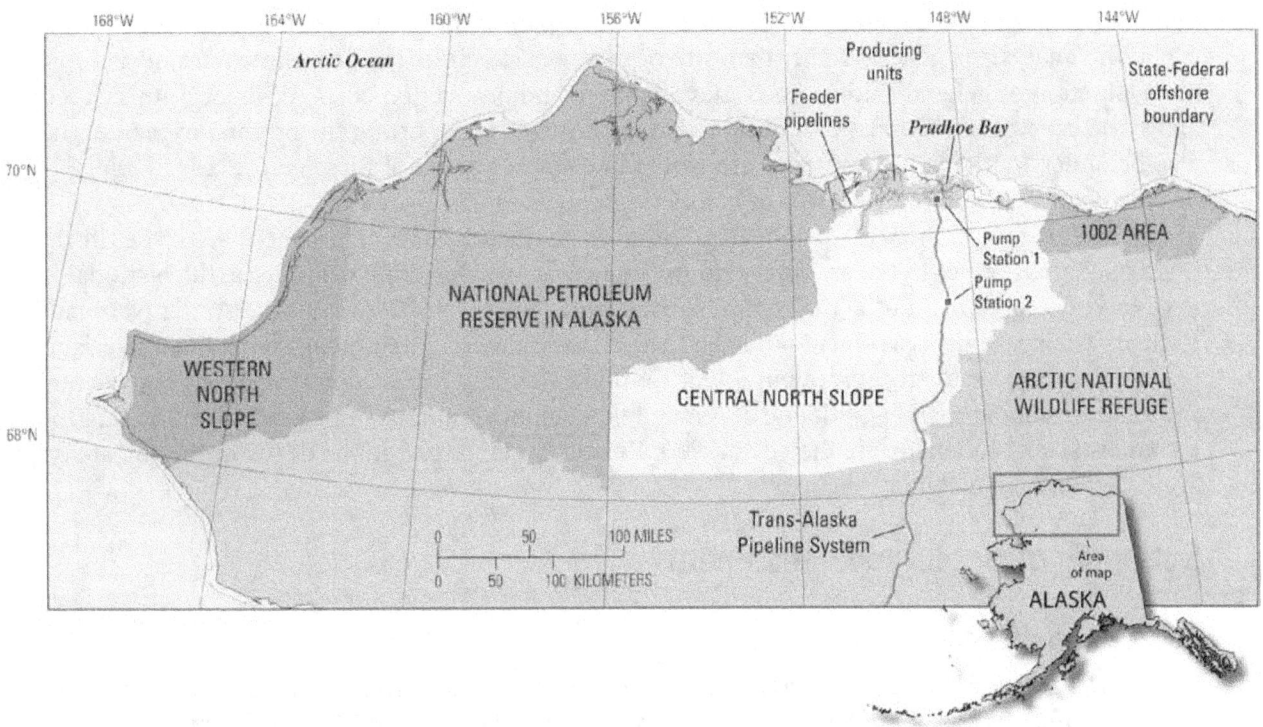

Figure 1. Map showing the Alaska North Slope assessment study area, which consists of Federal, Native, and State lands in the 1002 Area of the Arctic National Wildlife Refuge, the central North Slope, the National Petroleum Reserve in Alaska (NPRA), and the western North Slope (area west of the NPRA).

Geologic assessments predict the numbers and sizes of conventional oil and gas accumulations that could occur in the study area. The assessed oil and gas volumes in these undiscovered accumulations are called technically recoverable because they represent resources thought to be recoverable with current technology and are not linked to costs or product prices. For three of the four areas (but not the western North Slope), prices and costs required to transform the estimates of undiscovered technically recoverable resources into estimates of producible reserves were presented in separate reports at the time of publication of the original assessments.[1] The economic analysis prepared for this report is based on assessed resources represented by the four-area aggregation and updates in costs and technological and fiscal assumptions as of the end of 2007.

This economic analysis contains estimates of the part of the distribution of undiscovered accumulations that could be commercially developed at particular market prices. The prices must be sufficient to repay incremental costs of finding, developing, and producing oil and gas and transporting them to a market. Although the cost functions that are constructed show cost and resource-recovery possibilities and are not supply functions as defined by economists, the data that underlie the functions commonly provide the basis for market-supply models. This analysis does not predict the revenues (bonus payments or rentals for leases), nor does it attempt to estimate the regional or national secondary economic benefits that may result as a consequence of future development of the resource.

This report is intended to place the geologic resource analysis into an economic context that is informative and easily understood by decisionmakers. Resources that are not economic at the range of

---

[1]For the 1002 Area of the Arctic National Wildlife Refuge, see Attanasi (1999, 2005a,b); for the NPRA, see Attanasi (2003); and for the central North Slope, see Attanasi and Freeman (2005).

market prices considered are not expected to become part of the future reserve. The scope of the economic analysis is general rather than site or prospect specific. The economic analysis is limited to the evaluation of general finding costs, development and production costs (costs of primary recovery and some aspects of secondary recovery), and the costs of transporting the product to market. It should also be understood that the timing of the global industry's pursuit of these resources is largely determined by the expected returns of competing opportunities elsewhere.

In this report, the term "study area" refers to the North Slope assessment area (see fig. 1), and "study subareas" refer to the areas labeled in figure 1 as the western North Slope, the National Petroleum Reserve in Alaska, the central North Slope, and the 1002 Area of the Arctic National Wildlife Refuge. The geologic assessment procedures are first reviewed. A summary of the characteristics of the technically recoverable resources important for understanding the economic analysis is presented. Assumptions about markets, pricing, costs, and the technical relationships used in computing the incremental cost functions are then discussed. Results and interpretations of the economic analysis are presented in the concluding sections.

Synopsis of Geologic Assessment

Assessment Procedures

The North Slope geologic assessments are based on the concept of the petroleum play as the basic unit of assessment. A play is a set of known or postulated oil and (or) gas accumulations[2] sharing similar geologic, geographic, and temporal properties, such as source rock, migration patterns, timing, trapping mechanisms, or hydrocarbon type (Baker and others, 1984). On the basis of geologic knowledge, available seismic data, and the findings of past North Slope exploration, the assessment geologists defined and described the known and prospective petroleum plays. A total of 62 potential plays were assessed. Across all plays, the uniform minimum accumulation size for oil accumulations assessed is 20 million barrels (MMBO) of recoverable oil, and for natural gas accumulations, the minimum accumulation assessed is 250 billion cubic feet (BCF) of recoverable nonassociated natural gas.

For each play, the assessment geologists assigned subjective probabilities to the occurrence of hydrocarbon accumulations to capture play and prospect risk. The play probability (commonly called play risk) is the probability of occurrence of at least one accumulation of minimum size (20 MMBO recoverable oil or 250 BCF recoverable gas). For hypothetical plays where the assessor was not confident of the occurrence of at least one accumulation as large as the threshold size, the play probability was the product of the occurrence probability of the three play attributes of charge, trap, and timing.

A prospect probability was also assigned to each play. The prospect probability is the probability that any randomly chosen oil or gas prospect contains resources of at least 20 MMBO of technically recoverable oil or 250 BCF of technically recoverable gas. Prospect probabilities for oil and gas were generally different, but there was no attempt to assign different probabilities to individual prospects that might have been identified. The prospect probability may be computed as the product of the occurrence probabilities assigned by the geologist to the prospect attributes of charge, trap, and timing. The geologists also specified separate distributions for the number of oil and the number of gas prospects, as

---

[2]Accumulations are classified as either oil or nonassociated gas on the basis of their gas-to-oil ratios. Those having at least 20,000 cubic feet of gas per barrel of crude oil were classified as nonassociated gas; otherwise, the accumulations were classified as oil. Oil accumulations may have associated gas, and gas accumulations may have natural gas liquids.

well as reservoir depth. The number of accumulations (meeting the threshold size) is then the product of the number of prospects, the play probability, and the prospect probabilities.

Data from available field studies, regional geophysical studies, knowledge about regional trends, and postulated regional geologic history allowed the assessment geologists to specify probability distributions for the reservoir attributes of (1) net reservoir thickness, (2) area of closure, (3) porosity, (4) trap fill, and (5) reservoir depth. Numerically simulated values from these distributions were combined with the engineering-based reservoir equation[3] to predict size, depth, and characteristics of the undiscovered accumulations. These simulations, which were conditioned on the play and prospect probabilities, constituted the assessment results (see Schuenemeyer, 2005).

In order to properly aggregate play results, when expressed as probability distributions to the study-area level, the covariance among plays must be specified. Pairwise dependencies between plays of the hydrocarbon charge, trap, and timing play attributes were assigned by the assessment geologists to all 62 plays. The ranked dependencies (high, medium, low) were assigned correlation values, and the values were averaged so that the pairwise dependency between plays was reduced to one correlation value. The resulting correlation matrix was transformed to a covariance matrix that was used in the aggregation of play results to the study-area level. Details of the aggregation procedure were discussed in Schuenemeyer (2005).

Characteristics of Assessed Technically Recoverable Resources

Estimates of the total volume of resources are shown in table 1. At the mean values, 24.3 billion barrels of oil (BBO) was assessed in 179 oil accumulations and 103 trillion cubic feet (TCF) of nonassociated gas was assessed in 145 gas accumulations. At the mean, an additional 20.0 TCF of associated gas was estimated to be in undiscovered oil accumulations. The volumes of oil assessed for the NPRA and the 1002 Area of ANWR are about equal and together account for 86 percent of the oil assessed. Most of the remainder of the undiscovered oil was assigned to the central North Slope study subarea. More than 61 percent of the natural gas in gas accumulations was assigned to the NPRA. Table 1 also shows that the North Slope study area aggregation estimates at the 95th and 5th fractiles for oil in undiscovered oil accumulations are 17.4 BBO and 32.4 BBO, respectively, and for nonassociated gas (that is, gas in gas accumulations), they are 74.3 TCF and 135 TCF, respectively. The individual study-area volumes shown in the table for these fractiles represent each area's contribution to the aggregate North Slope fractile estimate.[4]

In the study subareas shown in figure 1, the assessment included onshore Federal, State, and Native lands and offshore State areas. The area represented by the NPRA accounts for 52 percent of the

---

[3]For each oil accumulation, for example, the simulated reservoir-attribute values included the following: (1) net reservoir thickness, t, in feet, (2) area of closure, ac, in thousands of acres, (3) porosity, p, as a decimal fraction, (4) trap fill, f, as a decimal fraction, and (5) hydrocarbon pore space, hps, as a function of p and S_w, where S_w is water saturation as a decimal fraction. The assessors provided estimates of the oil recovery factor, rf_o, as a fraction of the in-place resources that are recoverable, and the formation volume factor, fvf_o, was calculated as a function of trap depth and API gravity. Oil accumulation size, szo, in millions of barrels was calculated with the following equation:
$szo = 7.758(t)(hps)(f)(rf_o)(ac)/(fvf_o)$
where $hps = p(1-S_w)$.
For gas accumulations, the size, szg, in billions of cubic feet was computed as:
$szg = 4.356(t)(hps)(f)(rf_g)(ac)(fvf_g)*10^{-8}$
where the recovery factor and formation volume factor were specifically defined for gas accumulations.

[4]The area contributions to the aggregate North Slope study area 95th- and 5th-fractile estimates are generally not the same as the individual area's 95th- and 5th-fractile estimates.

total study area under consideration, the central North Slope accounts for 31 percent, the western North Slope 13 percent, and the 1002 Area of ANWR 4 percent.

Table 1.   Aggregate estimates of the technically recoverable volumes of conventional oil, natural gas, and natural gas liquids based on the mean, 95th-, and 5th-fractile estimates of oil and nonassociated gas, respectively, for the North Slope study area.

[NPRA, National Petroleum Reserve in Alaska; ANWR, Arctic National Wildlife Refuge; BBO, billions of barrels of oil; TCF, trillions of cubic feet of gas; BBL, billions of barrels of liquid. Data are from sources described in appendix 1]

Area	Oil accumulations			Gas accumulations	
	Oil (BBO)	Associated gas (TCF)	NGL (BBL)	Nonassociated gas (TCF)	NGL (BBL)
Mean value estimate					
NPRA	10.47	11.59	0.21	63.33	0.68
Central North Slope	3.41	3.60	0.08	25.10	0.29
1002 Area of ANWR	10.35	4.76	0.19	3.81	0.13
Western North Slope	0.08	0.05	0.00	10.36	0.12
Total study area	24.30	19.99	0.48	102.60	1.22
95th-fractile oil estimate for study area					
NPRA	8.55	9.50	0.17	62.77	0.68
Central North Slope	2.80	2.97	0.07	22.20	0.26
1002 Area of ANWR	5.92	2.67	0.10	3.19	0.08
Western North Slope	0.17	0.05	0.00	11.37	0.13
Total study area	17.44	15.19	0.34	99.53	1.15
5th-fractile oil estimate for study area					
NPRA	13.28	14.82	0.27	66.51	0.72
Central North Slope	3.87	4.12	0.09	26.80	0.31
1002 Area of ANWR	15.16	6.42	0.23	4.52	0.11
Western North Slope	0.09	0.04	0.00	10.44	0.11
Total study area	32.40	25.40	0.60	108.27	1.25
95th-fractile gas estimate for study area					
NPRA	9.87	11.01	0.20	45.60	0.49
Central North Slope	3.17	3.39	0.08	19.14	0.22
1002 Area of ANWR	10.39	5.15	0.23	3.47	0.11
Western North Slope	0.06	0.03	0.00	6.13	0.07
Total study area	23.48	19.58	0.50	74.34	0.89
5th-fractile gas estimate for study area					
NPRA	10.80	11.94	0.22	85.49	0.91
Central North Slope	3.68	3.86	0.09	33.09	0.38
1002 Area of ANWR	10.74	5.00	0.19	4.06	0.11
Western North Slope	0.06	0.04	0.00	12.40	0.14
Total study area	25.28	20.85	0.50	135.03	1.54

The total volume of the assessed undiscovered technically recoverable resource (both oil and gas) is significant relative to the recoverable resources in past discoveries (21.1 BBO, 35.4 TCF) in the Alaska Arctic Petroleum Province (Houseknecht and Bird, 2006). The super-giant Prudhoe Bay field, giant Kuparuk River field, and several other fields in the 500-MMBO range account for most of that discovered volume. Houseknecht and Bird (2006) listed a total of 38 oil and gas accumulations discovered through 2005. At the mean estimate, the assessed undiscovered volumes were posited to be in 324 (179 oil, 145 gas) accumulations, suggesting that future finds will be much smaller than past discoveries.

Table 2 shows the number of accumulations by size class and the corresponding percentage share of oil in oil accumulations and nonassociated gas in gas accumulations by size class. Figures 2*A* and 2*B* display the assessed oil and gas accumulation size distributions posited for assessed undiscovered accumulations at the 95th-fractile, the mean, and the 5th-fractile estimates, respectively. In the undiscovered oil accumulation size distributions, more than 95 percent of the oil accumulations are smaller than 1 BBO. At the 95th fractile, only three accumulations with a total of 2.4 BBO have sizes greater than 500 MMBO. At the mean and 5th-fractile estimates, oil in accumulations of at least 500 MMBO amounts to about 5.2 BBO (in six accumulations) and 9.3 BBO (in nine accumulations), respectively.

Figure 2*B* shows the gas accumulation size distributions. The gas accumulation size distribution data show a relatively small proportion of the gas resource in accumulations in sizes greater than 3 TCF (when converted to barrels of oil equivalent (BOE); 3 TCF is about the same as 500 MMBO because 1 BOE = 6,000 cubic feet of natural gas). Accumulations containing at least 3 TCF of gas account for only 4 percent of the assessed nonassociated gas at the 95th-fractile estimate, 12 percent of the gas at the mean estimate, and 19 percent of the gas at the 5th-fractile estimate (see table 2).

The size-frequency distributions of undiscovered oil and gas accumulations for the mean estimates were disaggregated to show the size distributions of undiscovered oil and gas accumulations for each study area. Figure 3*A* and figure 3*B* display undiscovered size distributions for oil accumulations and nonassociated gas accumulations, respectively. Table 3 shows the numerical frequencies, as well as the cumulative volume distributions, for mean estimates.

At the mean estimates, the NPRA and the 1002 Area have assessed oil volumes that are almost identical (see table 1), but they have quite different oil accumulation size distributions (see table 3). About 43 percent of the assessed oil for the 1002 Area is assigned to accumulations of at least 500 MMBO, whereas only 6 percent of the assessed NPRA oil is assigned to fields of that size. For the NPRA, the size class representing accumulations between 128 and 256 MMBO is posited to have the largest percentage (33 percent) of the oil. For the central North Slope, undiscovered oil accumulations of between 64 and 128 MMBO have the largest percentage (29 percent) of its assessed oil.

The distributions of natural gas accumulations in the four subareas (see table 3) are also quite different. In the NPRA, 15 percent of the total mean resource (9.7 TCF) is assigned to accumulations of at least 3 TCF in size. Table 3 shows that the largest gas volume (17.2 TCF) for the NPRA is assigned to the size class representing accumulations from 768 BCF to 1.54 TCF, whereas the largest gas volumes for the western North Slope and for the central North Slope are assigned to the next smaller size class (384 to 768 BCF). The posited gas field sizes are only modest by Arctic standards, and the likelihood of commercial development will depend on how closely they are clustered and how close they are to transportation infrastructure when it is built.

Table 2. Cumulative percentage distribution of estimated undiscovered technically recoverable oil in oil accumulations and nonassociated (NA) gas in gas accumulations by size class for the North Slope study area.

[MMBO, millions of barrels of oil; BBO, billions of barrels of oil; BCF, billions of cubic feet of gas; TCF, trillions of cubic feet of gas]

Oil in oil accumulations

Size class (MMBO)	95th-fractile estimate			Mean estimate			5th-fractile estimate		
	Number of accumulations	Oil in class (BBO)	Cumulative percent	Number of accumulations	Oil in class (BBO)	Cumulative percent	Number of accumulations	Oil in class (BBO)	Cumulative percent
4,096-8,192	0.0	0.0	0	0.0	0.1	0	0.0	0.0	0
2,048-4,096	0.0	0.0	0	0.2	0.6	3	0.8	2.3	7
1,024-2,048	0.6	0.8	4	1.2	1.6	9	2.0	2.7	15
512-1,024	2.4	1.6	14	4.4	3.0	22	6.4	4.4	29
256-512	11.6	4.1	37	16.7	5.8	45	21.5	7.5	52
128-256	27.1	4.8	65	33.7	6.1	70	42.2	7.7	76
64-128	37.7	3.4	85	45.4	4.2	87	50.8	4.7	90
32-64	42.8	2.0	96	48.8	2.3	97	51.8	2.4	97
20-32	28.7	0.7	100	31.2	0.8	100	34.0	0.9	100

Gas in nonassociated (NA) gas accumulations

Size class (BCF)	95th-fractile estimate			Mean estimate			5th-fractile estimate		
	Number of accumulations	NA gas in class (TCF)	Cumulative percent	Number of accumulations	NA gas in class (TCF)	Cumulative percent	Number of accumulations	NA gas in class (TCF)	Cumulative percent
24,576-49,152	0.0	0.0	0	0.0	0.0	0	0.0	0.0	0
12,288-24,576	0.0	0.0	0	0.0	0.7	1	0.1	2.0	1
6,144-12,288	0.1	1.3	2	0.4	3.4	4	1.2	10.3	9
3,072-6,144	0.4	1.7	4	2.0	8.4	12	3.2	13.6	19
1,536-3,072	5.2	10.4	18	8.3	16.9	29	11.7	24.1	37
768-1,536	20.3	20.9	46	25.8	27.1	55	31.1	33.2	62
384-768	46.7	25.0	80	55.2	29.5	84	61.7	33.4	86
250-384	49.1	15.1	100	53.6	16.5	100	59.8	18.4	100

8

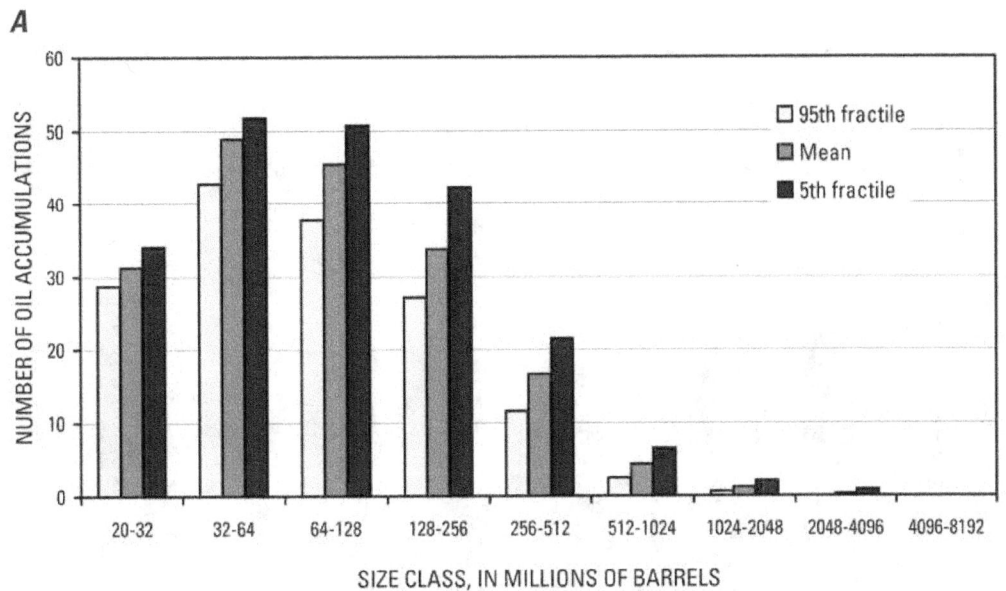

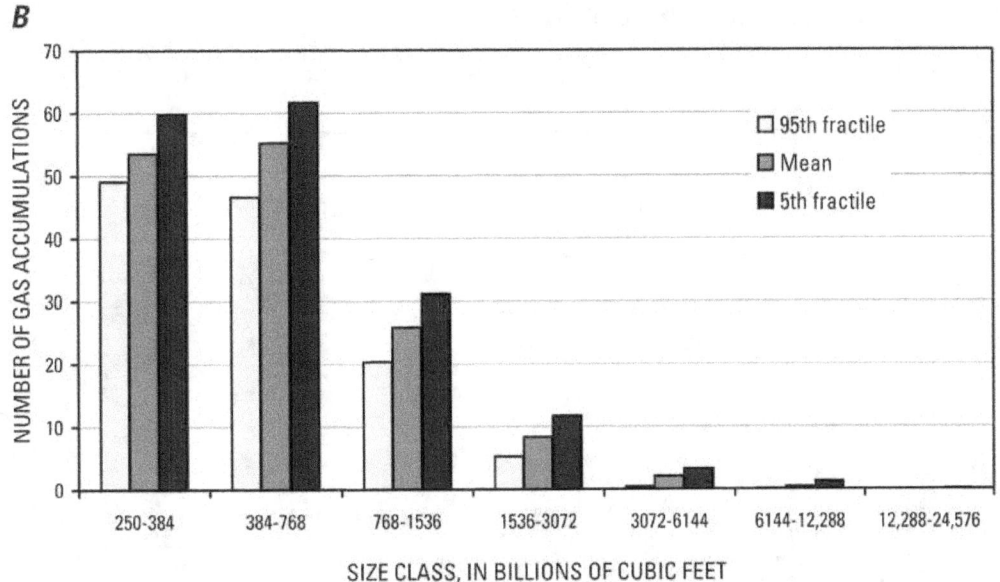

Figure 2. Graphs of the size-frequency distributions of the estimated number of accumulations of undiscovered (*A*) oil and (*B*) gas associated with the 95th-fractile, mean, and 5th-fractile volume resource estimates in the Alaska North Slope assessment study area.

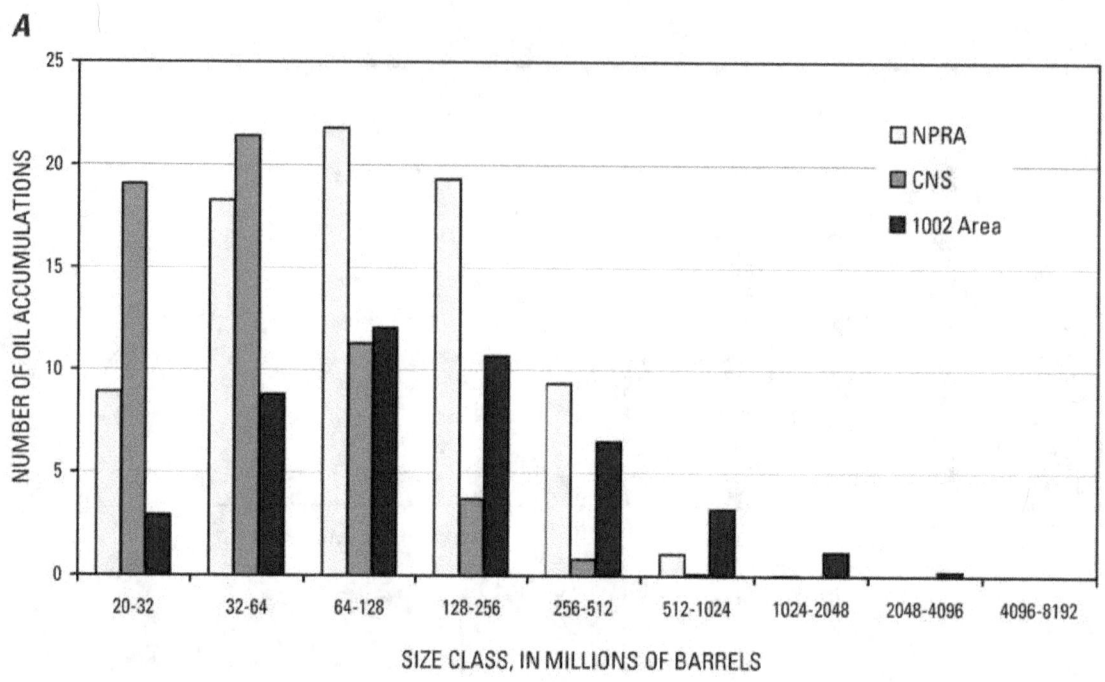

A

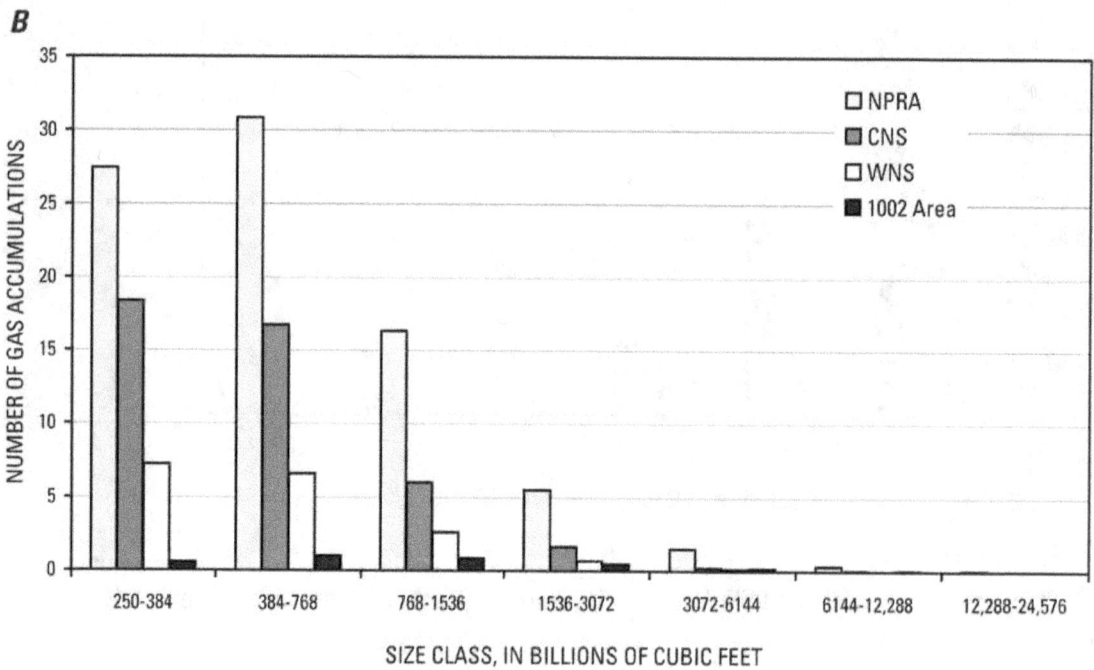

B

Figure 3. Graphs of the size-frequency distributions of the estimated number of accumulations of undiscovered (*A*) oil and (*B*) gas at the mean volume resource estimate by study subarea in the Alaska North Slope assessment study area. Oil assessed in the western North Slope (WNS) is so small that it would not be detectable in figure 3*A*. NPRA, National Petroleum Reserve in Alaska; CNS, central North Slope.

Table 3. Cumulative percentage distribution of mean estimates of undiscovered technically recoverable oil in oil accumulations and nonassociated gas in gas accumulations by size class for each North Slope study subarea.

[MMBO, millions of barrels of oil; BCF, billions of cubic feet of gas]

Size class (MMBO)	Number of accumulations	Oil in class (MMBO)	Class percent	Cumulative percent
National Petroleum Reserve in Alaska				
4,096-8,192	0.00	0	0	0
2,048-4,096	0.00	1	0	0
1,024-2,048	0.02	23	0	0
512-1,024	1.05	646	6	6
256-512	9.34	3,205	31	37
128-256	19.29	3,483	33	70
64-128	21.79	2,022	19	90
32-64	18.26	860	8	98
20-32	8.91	231	2	100
Central North Slope				
4,096-8,192	0.00	0	0	0
2,048-4,096	0.00	5	0	0
1,024-2,048	0.01	19	1	1
512-1,024	0.10	62	2	3
256-512	0.78	253	7	10
128-256	3.72	636	19	29
64-128	11.32	991	29	58
32-64	21.41	959	28	86
20-32	19.05	484	14	100
1002 Area of the Arctic National Wildlife Refuge				
4,096-8,192	0.01	56	1	1
2,048-4,096	0.22	572	6	6
1,024-2,048	1.16	1,587	15	21
512-1,024	3.22	2,263	22	43
256-512	6.51	2,318	22	66
128-256	10.65	1,929	19	84
64-128	12.08	1,120	11	95
32-64	8.78	419	4	99
20-32	2.94	77	1	100
Western North Slope				
4,096-8,192	0.00	0	0	0
2,048-4,096	0.00	2	2	2
1,024-2,048	0.00	4	6	8
512-1,024	0.01	5	6	14
256-512	0.02	8	11	24
128-256	0.08	13	18	42
64-128	0.20	18	24	65
32-64	0.39	18	23	89
20-32	0.34	9	11	100

Table 3. Cumulative percentage distribution of mean estimates of undiscovered technically recoverable oil in oil accumulations and nonassociated gas in gas accumulations by size class for each North Slope study subarea.—Continued

[MMBO, millions of barrels of oil; BCF, billions of cubic feet of gas]

Size class (BCF)	Number of accumulations	Gas in class (BCF)	Class percent	Cumulative percent
National Petroleum Reserve in Alaska				
24,576-49,152	0.00	0	0	0
12,288-24,576	0.04	630	1	1
6,144-12,288	0.36	2,801	4	5
3,072-6,144	1.52	6,316	10	15
1,536-3,072	5.50	11,272	18	33
768-1,536	16.35	17,218	27	60
384-768	30.85	16,614	26	87
250-384	27.43	8,483	13	100
Central North Slope				
24,576-49,152	0.00	0	0	0
12,288-24,576	0.00	7	0	0
6,144-12,288	0.03	186	1	1
3,072-6,144	0.22	894	4	4
1,536-3,072	1.65	3,335	13	18
768-1,536	6.02	6,217	25	42
384-768	16.74	8,811	35	77
250-384	18.37	5,650	23	100
1002 Area of the Arctic National Wildlife Refuge				
24,576-49,152	0.00	0	0	0
12,288-24,576	0.01	75	2	2
6,144-12,288	0.05	363	10	12
3,072-6,144	0.18	727	19	31
1,536-3,072	0.46	966	26	56
768-1,536	0.84	911	24	80
384-768	1.02	562	15	95
250-384	0.57	179	5	100
Western North Slope				
24,576-49,152	0.00	0	0	0
12,288-24,576	0.00	7	0	0
6,144-12,288	0.01	96	1	1
3,072-6,144	0.11	430	4	5
1,536-3,072	0.67	1,334	13	18
768-1,536	2.63	2,752	27	45
384-768	6.60	3,517	34	79
250-384	7.24	2,224	21	100

The aggregation procedure used the play simulation data (of play realizations) for its basic data. This procedure allowed recovery of the individual play realizations and hence accumulation size distributions that contributed to the study area volume fractile estimate, so the economic analysis could utilize the assessment geologists' allocations of the undiscovered resource to the economic zones defined and used in the earlier area studies; see figure 4 and appendix 2 of this report. The economic zones and resource allocations provide the conceptual basis for developing the costs associated with the existing and proposed product transportation system.

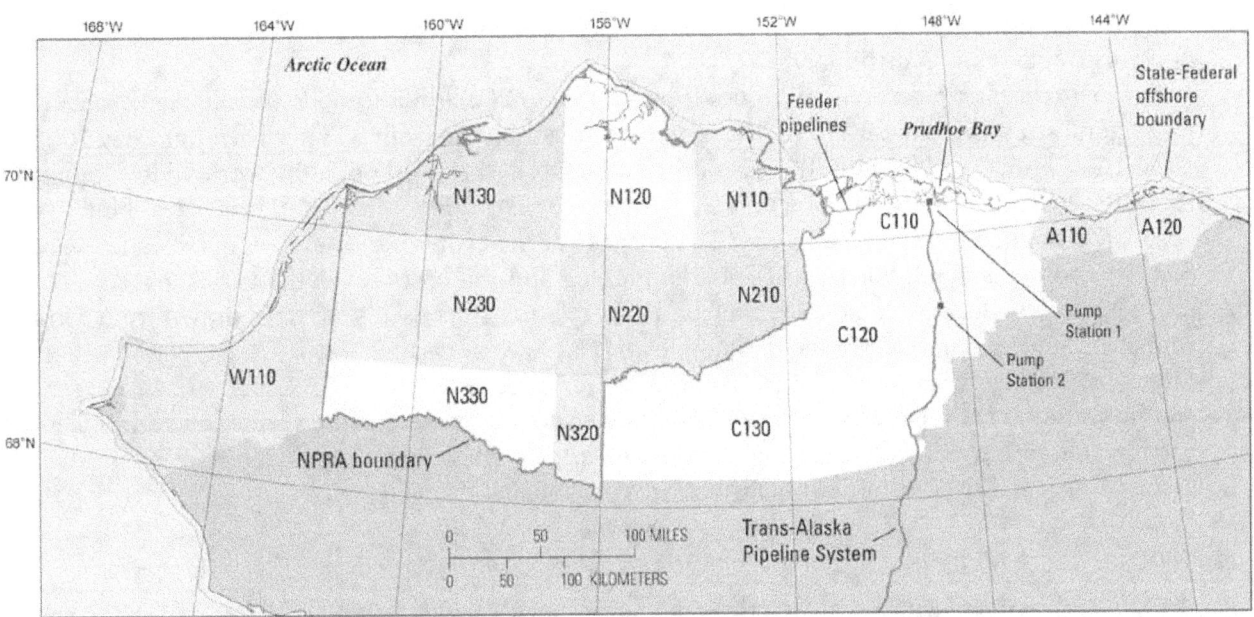

Figure 4. Map showing economic zones of the Alaska North Slope study area. Zone prefixes derive from names of the subareas, which are shown in figure 1: W, western North Slope; N, National Petroleum Reserve in Alaska (NPRA); C, central North Slope; and A, 1002 Area of the Arctic National Wildlife Refuge.

Economic Approach

Data

The geologic assessment data consisted of the play simulations (play realizations) associated with the North Slope study area 95th- and 5th-fractile volume estimates and the average of the play realizations that constituted the mean estimates. The simulation data include accumulation size, depth, reservoir net pay, and other characteristics. The data were partitioned into size and depth categories in order to characterize representative accumulations for the economic evaluation zones.

Major components of oil and gas industry costs, such as drilling and service industry costs, are affected by oil and gas price levels and changes that commonly follow economic cycles. Between early 2005 and July 2008, world market prices for crude oil moved from about $34 per barrel to nearly $150 per barrel. The oil and gas industry typically faces increasing costs when price increases, particularly if it tries to rapidly increase output.

For example, expansion of oil and gas production requires the development of new proved reserves.[5] Net additions to proved reserves generally necessitate an increase in the annual drilling rate. In the short run, say 36 months from the base period, unless there are idle drilling rigs and experienced crews, additional drilling demand will translate into increases in day rates for crews and drilling rigs, sometimes without any additional drilling actually taking place. Eventually, rates will rise sufficiently to expand the capacity of the drilling industry by the commissioning of new drill rigs and training of new crews, which constitutes a long-run adjustment. The commissioning of new and technically advanced rigs will expand industry capacity, leading to stable or slightly reduced drilling costs. If oil prices decline, drilling typically declines and only the most efficient rigs and crews will remain in the industry, allowing a reduction in drilling cost.

The recent rapid rise in oil prices from 2005 into 2008 produced significant cost escalation through most phases of operations. The amount of the increase from $34 per barrel in early 2005 to almost $150 per barrel in mid-2008 also drove all costs higher. Although the worldwide economic recession that seized most of the world's economies by late 2008 reduced oil prices by about two-thirds, costs have not declined symmetrically. The purpose of the economic assessment is to estimate resource recovery volumes in relation to cost, based upon the long-run costs of the industries that service the oil and gas sectors. Some of the engineering and cost relationships used here were drawn from earlier economic studies prepared for the individual study areas (Attanasi, 2003; Attanasi, 2005a; Attanasi and Freeman, 2005) and sources referred to in these references. IHS QUE$TOR software (IHS Inc., 2007) and information from James Craig (Minerals Management Service, written communication, 2008) were used in calibrating and updating some costs. A detailed explanation of engineering relationships, cost assumptions, and fiscal relationships is provided in appendixes 3 and 4.

Scope

Economic models are abstractions that characterize real economic systems and are typically just detailed enough to roughly approximate the outcomes of interactions between economic agents. Only the general direction and the approximate magnitude of the reaction of the system to price or cost change can be modeled. The results of the economic analysis are estimated costs of transforming undiscovered resources into discovered commercially producible volumes of oil and gas. Prices received by the operator must be sufficient to repay all investment expenditures, cover production costs including taxes, and still yield an acceptable return to investment; otherwise, the investment will not be undertaken. Costs include all expenditures incurred in finding, developing, and producing oil and gas resources and transporting them to market. The timing and costs associated with leasing that must precede exploration are not included. All these factors are highly uncertain because the posited oil and gas resources are still undiscovered.

The cost functions are time independent and should not be confused with the firm's supply or market-supply functions that relate marginal cost to production per unit time period. Because of the time-independent nature of the cost functions and the absence of market-demand conditions in the analysis, user costs and the opportunity costs of future resource use are not computed.

At any given price, the oil and gas industry will allocate funds over a number of provinces and worldwide sources of supply in order to meet market demand at lowest costs. Observed market price-supply relationships are the culmination of numerous supplier decisions over many projects and regions.

---

[5]Proved reserves are estimated quantities of hydrocarbons that geologic and engineering data demonstrate, with reasonable certainty, to be recoverable from identified pools under existing economic and operating conditions. Under normal circumstances, less than 20 percent of proved reserves (and often much less) can be extracted annually to avoid reservoir damage.

Incremental cost functions represent costs that are computed independently of activities in other areas. However, these cost functions and the data that underlie the functions are commonly used as the basis for market-supply models.

Economic Parameters

Technology and costs used in this analysis are assumed to represent those prevailing during the calendar year 2007.[6] As discussed above, the industries serving the oil and gas industry face erratic demands on services because of (1) volatile price changes related to shortfalls in production and (2) cost increases that are expected to be sustained despite new capacity that could modernize the service industries. The latter component is the primary basis for the cost assumptions in this economic analysis.

The oil prices evaluated in this economic analysis are based on the landed market prices at the west coast of the conterminous United States, which is the primary destination of oil produced in Alaska. The natural gas prices evaluated are those for gas delivered to Chicago or similar destinations in the northern U.S. Midwest, which is the likely market for North Slope gas. All transportation costs are subtracted from the assumed market prices to calculate the wellhead oil and gas prices used for project evaluation. The market prices are assumed to be sustained, rather than an erratic spot price. The market price of natural gas liquids is assumed to be 75 percent of the per-barrel price of crude oil.

The pipeline to transport natural gas to market in the conterminous United States has yet to be built. It is expected that the future gas pipeline will start near Pump Station 1 of the Trans-Alaska Pipeline System (TAPS) and proceed southward along the TAPS right of way until it is redirected to the southeast toward the Alberta Hub (AECO). The gas moving through the AECO market could reach U.S. markets through several northern border crossing points. Because of the uncertainty regarding the timing and access to shipping capacity of the future gas pipeline, this economic analysis includes data for two scenarios. For scenario 1, the assumption is that pipeline access for new discoveries will occur approximately 10 years from the time of discovery; for scenario 2, the assumption is that access will not occur until 20 years after discovery. The longer delay gives priority access for proven gas reserves in fields near the pipeline origin before new supplies are accepted from new outlying discoveries. For these scenarios, the expected net present values of commercial discoveries are discounted for the lag time between discovery and startup. To simplify the analysis, it is assumed that there is no direct cost to the operation as a result of delays (lease rental, storage, and reserve taxes) during the period between discovery and field development for market sales.

In recent years, market prices for natural gas have been very volatile, ranging mostly from $5/MCF to $12/MCF and, in some markets, climbing even higher. However, historically the market valuation of gas relative to crude oil on a calorific heating basis has been discounted. For the gas prices that are used in the valuation of potential gas discoveries, unless otherwise stated, gas is valued at the market at two-thirds the value of oil based on calorific heating value or British thermal units (Btu). Because of the sheer size of the investment required for pipeline construction ($30 billion), the pipeline owners are likely to require long-term contracts of shippers and buyers, who, in turn, will agree to pay stable shipping fees (tariffs). Associated gas in new oil discoveries is not valued at the market but is assumed to be stripped of liquids and re-injected into the oil accumulation for pressure maintenance.[7] Therefore, associated gas is not included in the gas cost functions.

---

[6]As noted above, costs were adjusted to represent the stable component.

[7]Associated gas could be recovered for sale when oil is depleted. However, the discounting for decades of delay in sales would significantly reduce its value so much that at the time of discovery, it would not be a significant factor in the decision to develop the oil discovery.

During 2007, domestic refiner acquisition cost for crude oil ranged from $50.77 to $85.29 per barrel. History has shown that when prices rise substantially and rapidly, it is unrealistic to assume that costs in constant dollars will match price increases and hold (Kuuskraa and others, 1987). In order to adjust cost to changes in prices, it is assumed that for market prices between $40 to $100 per barrel, the prevailing 2007 costs are unaffected by price volatility. Above $100 per barrel and below $40 per barrel, drilling, facilities, and operating costs would rise or decline as a fraction of the percentage price changes. Details of the price-cost adjustment are presented in appendix 3.

Discounted cashflow analysis is specific to an individual project, and tax preference items that might be important from a corporate accounting stance are not considered in this general economic assessment. A minimum 12 percent after-tax required return is applied to all projects that are deemed economic. A one-eighth royalty is assumed to be paid to the owner of the mineral rights. In this study, the assumption is that $0.25 per barrel of produced oil is set aside by operators to fund abandonment costs for oil fields and $0.05/MCF is set aside to fund the abandonment cost of natural gas fields. All pipelines outside the petroleum lease unit are assumed to be operated as common carriers with estimated tariffs that must repay annual operating costs, State property tax, State and Federal income taxes, and a 12 percent return to investors.

The Alaska State taxes include a corporate income tax, ad valorem tax (property tax), and petroleum production tax (called ACES[8]). Although the nominal corporate income tax rate is 9 percent, the effective tax rate is set by a complex formula based on the individual company's production and sales. For planning purposes, State agencies use effective rates between 2 and 4 percent of net income. An effective corporate tax rate of 4 percent is used here. The State's ad valorem tax is an annual charge equivalent to 2 percent of the economic value of equipment, facilities, and pipelines. The State petroleum production tax (ACES) replaced the severance tax and is described in appendix 4. Federal income tax provisions are as of the end of 2007[9] with an assumed rate of 35 percent of taxable income.

Economic Assumptions

For this study, it is assumed that industry will not invest in new projects unless the full operating costs, taxes, capital, and cost of capital can be recovered. The costs modeled here include all expenditures (except lease bonus and rental payments) that are estimated to be incurred by the industry in finding, developing, and producing the product and transporting it to market. Costs and market prices are modeled in constant 2007 dollars.[10]

Unless otherwise stated, it is assumed that all of the North Slope study area is available for exploration and development for oil and gas. Currently, the central North Slope and parts of the NPRA are open on a limited basis.

The cost functions presented are time independent, and so they are not the same as supply functions, which relate price to quantity per unit time. Because of the time-independent nature of the cost functions and the absence of market-demand conditions in the analysis, user costs or the opportunity costs of future resource use are not computed.

---

[8]ACES is an acronym for Alaska Clear and Equitable Share tax (also see Alaska Department of Revenue, Tax Division, 2007, for State tax explanation).

[9]According to the 1986 Tax Reform Act, 30 percent of development well drilling cost is classified as a tangible cost and therefore is capitalized over 7 years. Of the remaining 70 percent of drilling cost (that is, the intangible drilling costs), 30 percent is depreciated over 5 years and the remaining 70 percent is expensed immediately.

[10]A primary motivation of this analysis is to capture economic implications of geologic uncertainty. Therefore the economic variables and engineering relationships used are expressed as point estimates rather than as probability distributions.

Economic Procedures

A new discovery is commercially developable if the after-tax net present value of its development is greater than zero. Market prices, size, depth, regional costs, and co-product ratios determine whether a discovery will be commercially developable. The algorithm that calculated costs used the predicted size and depth distribution of undiscovered fields (at economic zone level) to compute quantities of resources that are commercially developable at various prices.

A finding rate model (Attanasi and Bird, 1996) was adjusted for each economic zone's undiscovered oil and gas accumulations and was used to forecast the size and depth distribution of new discoveries from increments of wildcat drilling. The results of the forecasts drive economic field development and production processes to establish the expected aggregate value of new discoveries. Specifically, at a given price, the commercial value of developing a representative oil or gas accumulation in a specific size class and depth category is determined by the results of a discounted cashflow (DCF) analysis.

The net after-tax cashflow consists of revenues from the production of oil less the operating costs, capital costs in the year incurred, and all taxes. All new discoveries from a size and depth category are assumed to be developed if the representative accumulation is commercially developable, that is, the after-tax DCF is greater than zero, where the discount rate (12 percent) represents the cost of capital and the industry's required return.

Production is assumed to stop (the economic limit is reached) when operator income declines below the sum of direct operating costs and the operator's production-related taxes. Commercially developable accumulations are summed and represent an estimate of the potential reserves attainable from undiscovered accumulations at a given price and required hurdle or minimum rate of return. The results from this procedure do not imply that every accumulation determined to be commercially developable is worth exploring for because some accumulations are predicted by the finding rate model that will only meet the commercially developable threshold and not repay finding costs.

Incremental units of exploration, development, and production effort will not be expended unless the revenues expected to be received from eventual production will cover the incremental costs, including a normal return on the incremental investment. Exploration continues until the incremental cost of drilling wildcat wells equals or exceeds the after-tax net present value of the commercial discoveries identified by the last increment of wildcat wells. For the last increment of hydrocarbons produced from a field, operating costs (including production-related taxes) per barrel of oil equivalent are equal to price. This procedure assures that for the commercially developable resources discovered by the last economic increment of wildcat wells, the sum of per-barrel finding, development, and production costs equals the wellhead price (price of oil to the field owner).[11]

When oil and gas accumulations occur in the same depth interval and geographic basin, exploration productivity is determined jointly by the expected oil and gas targets and their economic value. If the oil search finds gas and the gas discovery has a positive after-tax net present economic value, the operator might develop the gas or sell the discovery to an operator that will develop the discovery. However, if the gas discovery is of no value, the discovery is reported as a dry hole, with a show of gas. So, when oil and gas accumulations occur in the same exploration area and depth intervals, the expected number of wildcat wells depends on the net present values for both the oil and the

---

[11]The marginal finding costs as described here are calculated by dividing the cost of the last increment of wildcat wells (which is approximately equal to the sum of the after-tax net present value of all commercially developable fields discovered in that last increment of exploration) by the amount of economic resources discovered by the last increment of exploration. Marginal development and production cost per barrel (for the economic resources discovered in that last increment of exploration) are calculated by subtracting the marginal finding costs from the wellhead price.

nonassociated gas that are found. In such situations, the incremental cost function for oil discoveries depends on the value imputed to the gas finds and the incremental cost function for nonassociated gas depends on the valuation of the oil. This procedure of representing the joint nature of oil and gas exploration with finding rate functions has been applied to most U.S. provinces analyzed in the economic component of the 1995 U.S. Geological Survey's National Oil and Gas Assessment (Attanasi, 1998).

Cost Components

Transportation, Infrastructure, and Location Assumptions

Since 1977, oil produced in northern Alaska has been shipped via the Trans-Alaska Pipeline System (TAPS) to the Port of Valdez in southern Alaska and then transported by marine tanker to market. The peak flow for TAPS occurred in 1988 at just above 2.0 million barrels per day. For 2007, the TAPS flow rate averaged slightly less than 0.74 million barrels per day of oil and natural gas liquids. Pump capacity for the TAPS has recently been reduced so the apparent 1.25 million barrels per day of unused capacity is not currently available. The reduced capacity can be restored in the future if discoveries result in increased North Slope daily production. For this analysis, it is assumed that TAPS will be able to accept any additional supplies in the foreseeable future.

The TAPS tariff rates and marine transport rates to market are projected semiannually by the Alaska Department of Revenue, Tax Division (2007, 2008). The marine transport rate represents transport cost weighted by projected sales volumes to various destinations from Valdez to markets that have included the west coast of the conterminous United States, the Far East, and the U.S. Gulf of Mexico region. These rates are projected on an annual basis to 2018. The annual TAPS tariff forecasts by the Alaska Department of Revenue from 2006 through 2018 averaged $3.81 per barrel (nominal dollars). The State projections assumed that the announced future TAPS tariffs will be reduced by litigation. This litigation seeks to remove from the pipeline's rate base certain expenditures claimed for pipeline enhancement. Alternatively, if one uses the 2008 rate of $4.87 *as the basis for projecting required pipeline annual revenues* and then divides the annual forecast of North Slope production to 2018, the average tariff is $5.65 per barrel. Rather than assume that future tariffs will decline or that litigation will have no effect, we assume here that the 2008 tariff rate from Pump Station 1 to Valdez of $4.87 per barrel will prevail forward. The State projection of $1.61 per barrel for marine tanker transport to market is used, and so the total transport cost for crude oil to market is $6.48 per barrel.

For the evaluation of nonassociated natural gas discoveries, it is assumed that gas will be transported from the discovery to a new gas conditioning plant located near Pump Station 1 of TAPS. The calculation of the gasline tariff from the gas conditioning plant to market is based, in part, on the data presented by TransCanada (TransCanada, 2007) in its application to the State of Alaska for a license under the Alaska Gasline Inducement Act. The analysis shows that the maximum transport tariff (including gas conditioning) to the Alberta Hub (AECO) is $2.58 per million Btu or $2.88/MCF if one uses the conversion factor in TransCanada's application. At the time of the application, rates quoted to transport gas to the U.S. market (ConocoPhillips, 2007) averaged $1.06/MCF. These sources estimate the overall loss in sales gas volume transported due to fuel use at compressor stations to be about 11.5 percent. The total cost of gas delivered to U.S. markets is then estimated to be $4.42/MCF.

The study area was partitioned into the economic zones shown in figure 4. These zones were also defined in the earlier studies of the central North Slope (Attanasi and Freeman, 2005), the NPRA (Attanasi, 2003), and the 1002 Area (Attanasi, 2005a,b). The western North Slope constituted a single economic zone. Distances and the corresponding pipeline costs for field feeder lines and regional

18

pipelines to transport oil or nonassociated gas to the Pump Station 1 area of TAPS were computed as levelized tariffs based on the assumption that the lines are operated as common-carrier pipelines. The assumed regional pipeline capacities, which in large measure determine the tariff rates from the discovery to the Pump Station 1 area or the inlet of the proposed gas conditioning plant, depend on play resource volumes that are computed with the play percentage allocation (see appendix 2) devised by the assessment geologists.

The play percentage allocations to the various economic zones were based on the play outlines and supplemental information developed by geologists relating to the identification of gas- and oil-prone areas within plays. A centroid for oil and a centroid for gas within each subarea were located on the basis of the play data. Transport costs to the Pump Station 1 area were computed by using the distance from each economic zone product centroid to Pump Station 1 or the location of the inlet of the proposed gas conditioning plant. Appendix 3 provides distances and pipeline capacities used for each zone.

Exploration, Development, and Production Costs

North Slope exploration and field development procedures are designed to accommodate special requirements in the Arctic environment. Wildcat drilling typically occurs in the winter when temporary ice roads, ice pads, and ice airstrips can be constructed to support drilling activities. After the ice melts, there is no sign of the previous winter's activity. Seasonal instability of the permafrost requires construction of permanent gravel pads to support production drilling rigs, wells, and facilities. Production wells are drilled directionally from the pads to target depths and lateral locations up to several miles away from the pad. Gravel drilling pads commonly accommodate as many as 40 well collars[12] spaced at 10-foot intervals along with production equipment. Sidetrack and multilateral drilling of two or more wells using a single well collar enable more well completions to be made on individual drilling pads.

The remoteness of the targets, the cold Arctic climate, and the absence of infrastructure result in high initial exploration and development costs compared with costs for conterminous U.S. locations. With stand-alone field development, produced oil is processed at the field's central processing facility and the final product is transported from the periphery of the field to TAPS. Because commercial North Slope discoveries are large relative to onshore fields in other areas, the introduction of new technology to increase recovery produces large payoffs in volumes of oil, and so operators commonly introduce such technological innovations early in the development cycle. For example, the application of extended reach drilling has allowed production wells access to distant reaches of the reservoir (commonly up to 4 miles), sometimes eliminating the need for additional drilling pads or allowing satellite pool development from existing drilling pads. Because of this technology, it is assumed that any offshore accumulation in State waters can be developed from onshore with extended reach wells or with an artificial gravel island in shallow waters, which would not substantially increase the stand-alone field cost.

Field development costs include well drilling and completion costs and the cost of facilities. Actual field development costs depend on site-specific characteristics of prospects. In the process of developing generic cost functions, a number of simplifying assumptions were made to keep the economic analysis tractable. The simulation realizations representing the undiscovered accumulations were grouped into accumulation size categories (table 2 provides the field size classes) and into 5,000-foot depth intervals. The analysis also included the costs of vertical delineation wells for each

---

[12]The well collar is at the end of the steel well casing that protrudes at the surface of the drilling pad.

19

accumulation evaluated. Development costs for a representative accumulation for each size and depth class were estimated and tested against an economic screen. If the representative accumulation was tested to be economic, then all accumulations in that size and depth category were considered commercially developable.

The actual costs associated with exploration and development drilling and construction of facilities depend on distance to existing infrastructure, remoteness to coastal staging points, and cost-sharing arrangements. For each economic zone, cost factors were used to adjust costs for the remoteness and lack of infrastructure relative to the costs thought to prevail in coastal areas of the central North Slope economic zone.

Exploration Costs

Costs of geologic and geophysical studies to locate exploration wells after a lease is acquired are included as part of the costs of wildcat wells. Wildcat well drilling costs were assumed to be twice the cost of drilling production wells for the particular economic zone. Nondrilling exploration expenditures include geologic and geophysical data collection after lease acquisition, scouting costs, and overhead charges. Nondrilling exploration expenditures,[13] exclusive of lease bonuses and lease rental, were assumed to amount to 50 percent of the wildcat well drilling costs (Vidas and others, 1993) and were added to wildcat exploration expenditures.[14] Exploration was evaluated in increments of 20 wildcat wells. Actual exploration and development costs will depend on site-specific characteristics of the prospects. Because play analysis does not provide specific locations, generic costs were used to model expenditures in each economic zone. Exploration costs are discussed further in appendix 3.

Development Costs for Crude Oil Accumulations

The two principal field development cost categories are (1) drilling and completion costs of production and injection wells and (2) facilities costs. Research on new procedures, materials, and technology target these two categories to reduce cost and (or) increase productivity. The use of horizontal wells for all development at the Alpine field was designed to enhance well productivity and enabled the commercial development of an accumulation with a relatively thin pay interval by North Slope standards (Gingrich and others, 2001). Greater well productivity reduces the required number of wells for field development and also reduces the size and (or) number of drilling pads. Because of existing infrastructure in the central North Slope, opportunities exist for facility sharing, which reduces the economic threshold for smaller discoveries.

Estimates of the number of development wells for a typical prospect assumed that the conventional well drainage area is 160 acres. Oil well recovery for the accumulation was based on the simulated reservoir attributes (see footnote 3 where the area variable, ac, is set equal to 160 acres). Details of the vertical well drainage area conversion for field designs with horizontal well configurations along with the procedure of drilling cost estimation are discussed in appendix 3.

Facilities include drilling pads, flow lines from drilling sites, the central processing unit, and infrastructure required for housing workers and storage. Facilities design and costs depend on peak fluid flow rates and ultimately on the field size. Although little information is in the public domain, a version

---

[13]For potential prospect identification, the three-dimensional (3-D) seismic expense may range from $750,000 to $1 million per prospect (David Houseknecht, U.S. Geological Survey, written communication, 2005). The 3-D seismic surveys would follow lease acquisition and depend on an existing 2-D seismic survey that located the prospect.

[14]For example, a typical vertical development well at a measured depth of 7,500 feet costs $6 million. Total costs for a comparable wildcat well where nondrilling costs amount to 50 percent of drilling cost are about $18 million, that is, the product of $6 million x 2(wildcat factor) x 1.5(nondrilling cost factor).

of the Northstar development plan, including development cost estimates, was submitted by British Petroleum Exploration to the State of Alaska for evaluation with its request for relief of profit-sharing provisions of the State lease (British Petroleum Exploration, 1996). Facilities costs were initially estimated for a region similar to the central North Slope by using the QUE$TOR cost analysis software (IHS Inc., 2007). These estimates were checked using facilities cost estimates inferred from published reports for other fields under development. The (step) cost relationship estimated for facilities is expressed as a per-barrel function of expected field recovery.

As of the end of 2007, the eight oil fields developed on a stand-alone basis in northern Alaska were Prudhoe Bay, Kuparuk River, Lisburne, Milne Point, Endicott, Badami, Northstar, and Alpine. Other developed fields and pools have produced fluids (oil, gas, and water) transported to the central processing unit of a nearby stand-alone field for separation. Point McIntyre, Niakuk, North Prudhoe Bay, and West Beach all use the central processing facilities of the Lisburne field. Prudhoe Bay production facilities process production from Midnight Sun, Aurora, Polaris, Borealis, and Orion. The Kuparuk River field facilities also process production from Tabasco, Tarn, Meltwater, and Palm. The oil produced from the Oooguruk unit operated by independent Pioneer Natural Resources is processed at the Kuparuk facilities.

The cost reduction from facility sharing depends on physical production configurations and on the relative bargaining strength of the satellite owner in comparison to that of the owner of the central processing facilities. The State of Alaska recognizes the importance of reducing capital barriers to attract entry of additional firms to the North Slope. The State has begun to study the potential regulatory issues of fair treatment of new entrants (Kaltenbach and others, 2004). Facilities sharing is assumed for smaller discoveries in economic zones C110 and N110 (see fig. 4). To minimize the development footprint within the 1002 Area, it is assumed that a shared oil and gas processing facility will be located just outside the 1002 Area (see Attanasi, 2005a,b, for details). Additional discussion is provided in appendix 3.

Production Profiles and Operating Costs for Crude Oil Accumulations

The oil accumulation production profiles assumed in this study are based on historical experience and on information supplied to the State of Alaska Oil and Gas Conservation Commission for support of the operator's development plans for new discoveries. Oil field operating costs include labor, supervision, overhead and administration, communications, catering, supplies, consumables, well service and workovers, facilities maintenance and insurance, and transportation. Annual field operating costs were estimated as a function of hydrocarbon and water fluid volumes and number of operating wells (Craig, 2002). The fluid volumes were projected annually from field production forecasts based on the relationship between water cut and cumulative production (see appendix 3). Water cut is the ratio of water produced compared to total volume of liquids produced. As fields are depleted, the water cut increases, thus increasing the per-barrel cost of oil processed. Operating cost estimates were reconciled with independently derived estimates using the QUE$TOR software.

Development Costs for Gas Accumulations

Although large natural gas accumulations have been discovered on the North Slope, natural gas has not been developed for commercial export from the North Slope because there is no gas transportation system to market. Currently 8 billion cubic (BCF) feet per day is recovered during oil production operations and 200 BCF per year is used as fuel. When a gas pipeline is constructed [2018 at the earliest (TransCanada, 2007)], most of the gas supplied to fill the pipeline will likely come from

Prudhoe Bay and other fields in the central North Slope subarea. Known gas reserves in these fields could supply the pipeline for at least 10 years if the nominal flow rate were 4.5 BCF per day.

Without any direct information about technical relationships or cost for gas development on the North Slope, the cost estimates developed for this study relied on the data generated from the QUE$TOR software for facilities cost and operating costs. Facilities costs include gas dehydration and, if required, acid removal but not a natural gas liquids plant. This analysis assumes that natural gas liquids are transported with the gas from the field through feeder lines to the regional line. The high-pressure regional lines transport gas and NGL in a dense phase to the gas processing facility to be constructed near Pump Station 1.

Gas well drilling and completion costs are assumed to be similar to oil drilling costs on a measured depth basis. The number of wells required to produce a new gas discovery was computed by assuming a well drainage area of 640 acres (National Petroleum Council, 1981a,b). It was assumed that the natural gas wells would be vertical or slightly deviated, but not horizontal.

Production Profiles and Operating Costs for Gas Accumulations

The production profiles of more recent discoveries in the Gulf of Mexico served as analogs for North Slope gas production. Development of North Slope gas discoveries is assumed to be delayed until the gas is marketable, that is, deliverable to market via a pipeline.[15] Production data from the "Significant oil and gas fields of the United States" database (Nehring Associates, Inc., 2004) for recent Gulf of Mexico fields were analyzed to determine the relationship between peak production of gas fields and their known recoverable gas by field size categories. With these peak production rates as a function of estimated field size, it was assumed that field production would be held constant until 75 to 80 percent of the field's original reserves was produced. The phase of constant production is then followed by a rapid decline at a rate of 24 percent per year. Annual production costs relied upon cost estimates developed using the QUE$TOR software (IHS Inc., 2007). Details are presented in appendix 3.

Economic Analysis Results

It is reasonable for firms to expend funds to identify an asset that is expected to have value at some future but uncertain date. For the North Slope's undiscovered gas, a key question is the timing of construction of the pipeline. There is the additional uncertainty about availability of pipeline capacity for transporting newly discovered gas to market. During a nominal 25-year life of the pipeline, which is planned to move 4.5 BCF per day, more than 41 TCF would be transported to market.[16] Estimates of the volumes of proven, pipeline-quality, conventional gas resources on the North Slope are about 30 to 33 TCF[17] (Thomas and others, 2007). These volumes suggest that additional discovered gas reserves will be required to support a viable pipeline over its design life.

To investigate the effect of timing on the economics of new gas developments, two scenarios were considered. Because the incremental cost functions are time independent, scenarios are static and represent resource costs at a single instant in time. For scenario 1, it is assumed that the scale and the regulation of the North Slope gas pipeline will allow some newly discovered gas to be transported to market upon completion of the pipeline. However, the current after-tax net present value of a new gas

---

[15]Even if a pipeline were operational by 2018, the earliest date discussed by TransCanada (2007), there might not be capacity for newly discovered gas until 10 years after the start of the gas pipeline's operation.

[16]A more likely useful life is 35 years (Thomas and others, 2007), during which the pipeline could transport more than 57 TCF of gas.

[17]The largest accumulations of discovered gas are attributed to Prudhoe Bay and Point Thompson (Thomas and others, 2007). At the current rate of gas usage (200 BCF per year), the gas available to the pipeline should be reduced by 2 TCF.

discovery is discounted for the 10-year period of pipeline permitting and construction. Specifically, the analysis shows how the incremental cost function appears to an operator who explores in 2008 and must discount the net present value of a find (based on constant cost and the assumed North Slope gas pipeline tariff) for the 10-year lag time between disbursement of exploration cost and projected cashflow. The projected cashflow streams consist of expenses associated with exploration and development and net revenue from production.

Scenario 2 assumes a 20-year delay between discovery and projected cashflow streams, but the development schedule is the same as that in scenario 1. Scenario 2 recognizes that the delay for development of newly discovered gas fields could lengthen an additional 10 years if proven gas in operating oil fields is given absolute priority for the capacity of the yet-to-be-built North Slope gas pipeline.

Estimated Economic Oil in Undiscovered Oil Accumulations

Table 4 shows results of the economic analysis, where the recoverable volumes are related to costs for the entire area. The economic effects of geologic uncertainty are clear by observing the differences in the cost functions evaluated using the field size distributions associated with the 95th- and 5th-fractile estimates (spanning the 90 percent confidence interval associated with the geologic estimates of technically recoverable resources). This set of estimates for the North Slope study area assumes that sales of gas in gas discoveries are delayed by 10 years after discovery and that there are no sales of associated gas in oil discoveries. At the mean assessment value estimate and a market price of $72 per barrel, it is estimated that 21.0 BBO of oil is economic to find, develop, and produce given the numerous assumptions discussed above. At $72 per barrel[18] at the 95th- and 5th-fractiles estimates for assessed oil in undiscovered oil accumulations, the estimated economic volumes amount to 14.5 BBO and 28.8 BBO, respectively. Alternatively at a price of $42 per barrel, the estimated economically recoverable oil is 8.8 BBO, 14.9 BBO, and 21.5 BBO at the 95th-fractile, mean, and 5th-fractile estimates and, similarly, at $108 per barrel, the estimated economically recoverable oil is 15.5 BBO, 22.2 BBO, and 30.3 BBO, respectively.

Figure 5A shows the associated functions graphically. The vertical lines indicate the assessed volumes of technically recoverable oil. The predicted volume resulting from the $30-per-barrel increase in prices from $42 to $72 per barrel was much greater than the volume response from $72 to $108 per barrel. However, over the long term, sustained high prices are likely to lead to improvements in recovery technology that will improve the recovery factor and shift the vertical lines to the right.

---

[18]The year of 2008 has been chaotic in terms of oil prices. EIA projects average refiner acquisition price for 2008 to be just over $72 per barrel (Energy Information Administration, 2008).

Table 4. Volumes of oil, associated gas, and natural gas liquids (NGL) from undiscovered oil accumulations, estimated for the entire North Slope study area, available as a function of specified market prices that offset costs of finding, developing, producing, and transporting the oil to market.

[Volumes represent the 95th-fractile, mean, and 5th-fractile estimates of undiscovered oil accumulations based on the North Slope study area aggregation consisting of all State, Federal, and Native lands in the National Petroleum Reserve in Alaska (NPRA), the central North Slope, the 1002 Area, and the western North Slope. Results of computations shown in the table are based on the assumption that sales of gas in gas discoveries are delayed 10 years. Prices are in 2007 dollars. Asc. gas, associated gas; $/bbl, dollars per barrel; BBO, billions of barrels of oil; TCF, trillions of cubic feet of gas; BBL, billions of barrels of natural gas liquids]

Oil price ($/bbl)	95th-fractile estimate			Mean estimate			5th-fractile estimate		
	Oil (BBO)	Asc. gas (TCF)	NGL (BBL)	Oil (BBO)	Asc. gas (TCF)	NGL (BBL)	Oil (BBO)	Asc. gas (TCF)	NGL (BBL)
27	2.71	0.92	0.02	5.63	1.83	0.03	10.02	3.27	0.06
30	3.11	1.07	0.02	7.48	3.23	0.07	12.31	4.72	0.11
33	5.43	3.31	0.07	10.14	5.79	0.14	15.50	7.15	0.18
36	6.32	4.12	0.08	11.43	6.97	0.18	17.01	8.36	0.22
39	7.22	4.93	0.11	12.95	8.50	0.22	19.18	10.13	0.26
42	8.78	6.23	0.13	14.93	10.67	0.27	21.51	12.14	0.30
45	10.09	7.33	0.15	16.26	12.01	0.31	23.63	14.08	0.34
48	11.45	8.38	0.16	17.44	13.30	0.33	24.63	15.03	0.36
51	11.85	8.76	0.17	18.19	14.06	0.35	25.51	15.90	0.38
54	12.29	9.10	0.17	18.97	14.94	0.37	26.32	16.56	0.40
57	13.02	9.70	0.18	19.41	15.44	0.38	26.91	17.09	0.41
60	13.21	9.91	0.19	19.76	15.82	0.39	27.59	17.77	0.42
63	13.68	10.34	0.19	20.39	16.46	0.40	27.93	18.06	0.43
66	13.75	10.40	0.19	20.66	16.78	0.41	28.33	18.39	0.44
69	14.28	10.85	0.20	20.78	16.91	0.41	28.52	18.55	0.44
72	14.47	11.04	0.20	21.03	17.18	0.42	28.76	18.80	0.45
75	14.57	11.13	0.20	21.21	17.37	0.42	29.15	19.12	0.45
78	14.78	11.30	0.20	21.40	17.56	0.43	29.31	19.24	0.46
81	14.80	11.32	0.20	21.42	17.59	0.43	29.40	19.33	0.46
84	14.99	11.48	0.21	21.66	17.80	0.43	29.50	19.40	0.46
87	15.08	11.54	0.21	21.86	18.00	0.43	29.74	19.59	0.46
90	15.24	11.67	0.21	21.88	18.02	0.43	29.81	19.65	0.46
93	15.26	11.68	0.21	21.98	18.12	0.44	29.93	19.74	0.46
96	15.34	11.74	0.21	22.10	18.22	0.44	29.98	19.78	0.47
99	15.47	11.83	0.21	22.14	18.25	0.44	30.03	19.82	0.47
102	15.48	11.83	0.21	22.18	18.29	0.44	30.15	19.89	0.47
105	15.49	11.84	0.21	22.19	18.30	0.44	30.20	19.92	0.47
108	15.50	11.85	0.21	22.19	18.30	0.44	30.28	20.00	0.47
111	15.55	11.90	0.21	22.25	18.34	0.44	30.33	20.05	0.47
114	15.61	11.94	0.21	22.29	18.38	0.44	30.34	20.05	0.47
117	15.70	12.00	0.21	22.40	18.48	0.44	30.35	20.06	0.47
120	15.77	12.06	0.21	22.48	18.55	0.45	30.42	20.11	0.47
123	15.77	12.06	0.21	22.48	18.56	0.45	30.42	20.11	0.47
126	15.81	12.08	0.21	22.49	18.56	0.45	30.51	20.17	0.47
129	15.81	12.08	0.21	22.52	18.58	0.45	30.54	20.18	0.47
132	15.87	12.11	0.21	22.53	18.59	0.45	30.61	20.23	0.48

Table 4. Volumes of oil, associated gas, and natural gas liquids (NGL) from undiscovered oil accumulations, estimated for the entire North Slope study area, available as a function of specified market prices that offset costs of finding, developing, producing, and transporting the oil to market.—Continued

[Volumes represent the 95th-fractile, mean, and 5th-fractile estimates of undiscovered oil accumulations based on the North Slope study area aggregation consisting of all State, Federal, and Native lands in the National Petroleum Reserve in Alaska (NPRA), the central North Slope, the 1002 Area, and the western North Slope. Results of computations shown in the table are based on the assumption that sales of gas in gas discoveries are delayed 10 years. Prices are in 2007 dollars. Asc. gas, associated gas; $/bbl, dollars per barrel; BBO, billions of barrels of oil; TCF, trillions of cubic feet of gas; BBL, billions of barrels of natural gas liquids]

Oil price ($/bbl)	95th-fractile estimate			Mean estimate			5th-fractile estimate		
	Oil (BBO)	Asc. gas (TCF)	NGL (BBL)	Oil (BBO)	Asc. gas (TCF)	NGL (BBL)	Oil (BBO)	Asc. gas (TCF)	NGL (BBL)
135	15.87	12.11	0.21	22.57	18.63	0.45	30.68	20.29	0.48
138	15.90	12.15	0.22	22.65	18.69	0.45	30.68	20.29	0.48
141	15.90	12.15	0.22	22.66	18.70	0.45	30.69	20.30	0.48
144	16.03	12.25	0.22	22.69	18.73	0.45	30.70	20.30	0.48
147	16.03	12.25	0.22	22.72	18.75	0.45	30.72	20.32	0.48
150	16.08	12.29	0.22	22.74	18.78	0.45	30.75	20.34	0.48

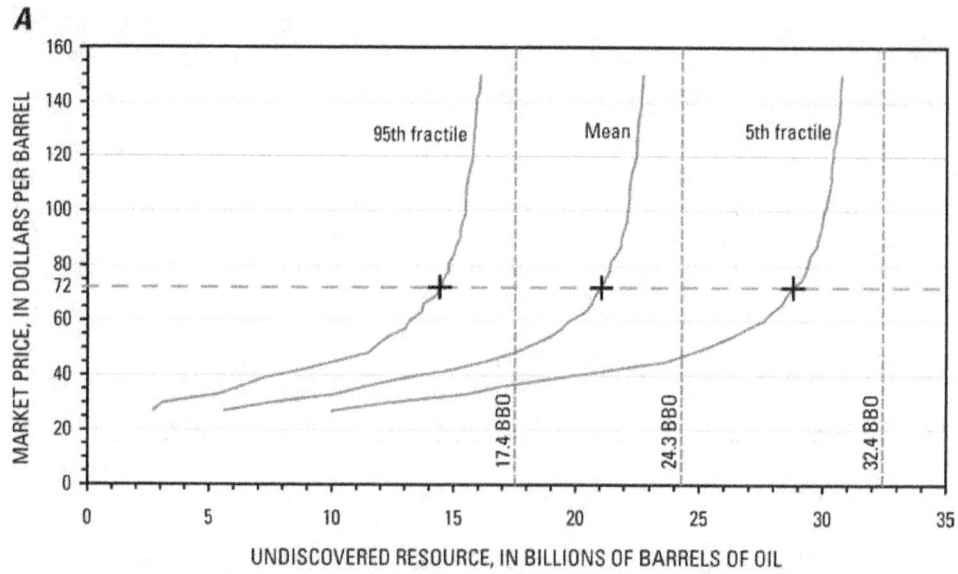

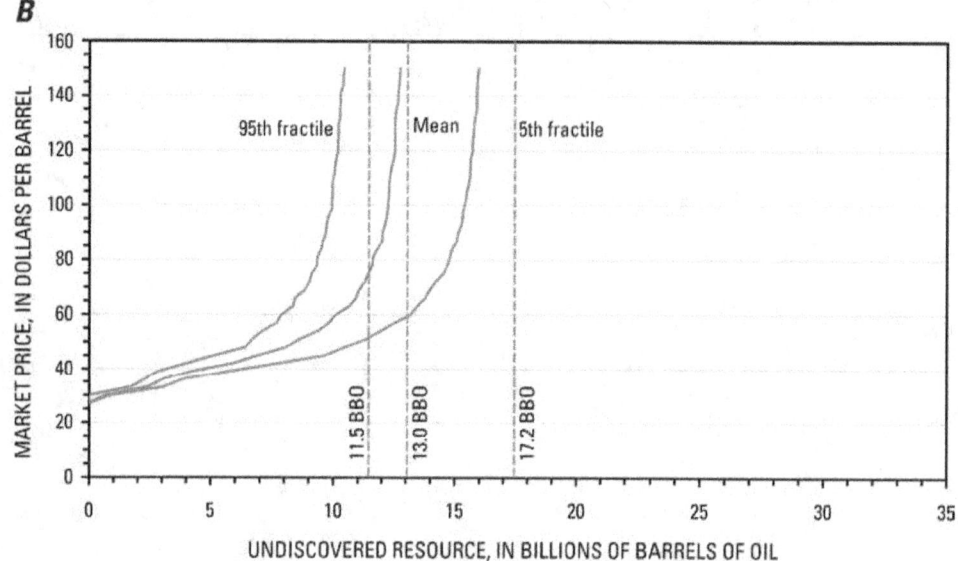

Figure 5. Summary graphs of undiscovered economic oil resources in (*A*) the entire North Slope study area and (*B*) the North Slope study area excluding the 1002 Area of the Arctic National Wildlife Refuge. Each red curve relates the market price (in 2007 U.S. dollars) to the estimated volume of economic resources where gas is valued at two-thirds the value of oil and the present value of gas accumulations is discounted for a 10-year delay; the green dashed vertical bars represent the volumes of technically recoverable oil, providing upper limits to the volume of economically recoverable oil. Thus, for the entire North Slope study area (*A*), at a market price of $72 per barrel (orange dashed horizontal line), at the 95th-fractile resource estimate representing a 95 percent occurrence probability of at least 17.4 billion barrels of oil (BBO), 14.5 BBO is economic. Similarly, at the 5th-fractile estimate representing a 5 percent occurrence probability of at least 32.4 BBO, 28.8 BBO is economic; at the mean estimate of 24.3 BBO, 21.0 BBO is economic.

The 1002 Area of the Arctic National Wildlife Refuge has been closed for any type of oil and gas activity for decades, although it is the only part of the refuge that was given special status whereby the prohibition of oil and gas exploration could be removed. Recognizing the longstanding prohibition on oil and gas activities, the estimates for economic oil shown in table 5 did not incorporate the resources assigned to the 1002 Area. At $72 per barrel, economic oil volumes at the 95th-fractile, the mean, and the 5th-fractile resource estimates are predicted to be 9.0 BBO, 11.3 BBO, and 14.2 BBO, respectively. Alternatively, at $42 per barrel, the economic oil volumes at the 95th-fractile, the mean, and the 5th-fractile estimates are predicted to be 4.0 BBO, 5.9 BBO, and 7.7 BBO, respectively, and at $108 per barrel, corresponding estimates of economic oil are 10.0 BBO, 12.3 BBO, and 15.6 BBO, respectively. Figure 5B shows the data displayed in table 5 graphically.

At $42 per barrel, from 35 to 45 percent of the technically recoverable oil (see table 1) in areas outside the 1002 Area is economic while 80 to 90 percent of the oil in the 1002 Area is economic. According to table 5, for areas outside of the 1002 Area, the lowest price at which it is economic to initiate exploration is about $30 per barrel at the mean and 5th-fractile estimates. The threshold price to initiate exploration in the 1002 Area is around $21 and $20 per barrel for undiscovered resources represented by the mean and 5th-fractile estimates, respectively.

Estimated Economic Gas in Undiscovered Gas Accumulations

Table 6 and figure 6 show estimates of the undiscovered economically recoverable gas in nonassociated gas accumulations assuming a 10-year and also a 20-year delay between disbursement of exploration expenditures and project startup. These scenarios model the current situation where construction of a major gas pipeline from the North Slope is not expected for 10 years. After the pipeline is operational, proven gas reserves at Prudhoe Bay could fill the pipeline for another 10 years, implying a 20-year delay. At $8/MCF (equivalent to $72/barrel oil market price) the economic nonassociated gas resources at the 95th-fractile, mean, and 5th-fractile estimates are predicted to be 10.8 TCF, 16.8 TCF, and 31.9 TCF, respectively. At the equivalent of a $42/barrel oil price, $4.67/MCF, it is not economic to explore for and develop undiscovered gas accumulations. At $12/MCF ($108/barrel), the economic nonassociated gas resources at the 95th-fractile, mean, and 5th-fractile estimates in gas accumulations are 40.7 TCF, 62.4 TCF, and 91.1 TCF, respectively. At $8/MCF, a 20-year delay reduces the economic nonassociated gas at the mean estimate to 14.4 TCF from 16.8 TCF (a 15 percent reduction). At $12/MCF, a 20-year delay reduces economic gas at the mean estimate to 45.3 TCF from 62.4 TCF (a 27 percent reduction). The results illustrate how uncertainties in access to pipeline capacity for new discoveries produce incentives to delay exploration expenditures. Furthermore, uncertainty in the sizes of the potential economic resources, in turn, directly affects the size of the pipeline to be built.

At the mean estimate, the 1002 Area of ANWR accounted for 43 percent of the undiscovered crude oil in the North Slope study area, but the 1002 Area accounts for less than 4 percent of the North Slope study area's nonassociated gas. The geologic underpinnings of these estimates are provided in detail in the U.S. Geological Survey 1998 assessment (Bird, 1999). If this gas assessment is correct, then the effects of prohibiting exploration on total economic gas would be small if the 1002 Area were removed from table 6.

Table 6 also shows the volumes of natural gas liquids (NGL) that could be recovered during production of nonassociated gas. Although the fractions of NGL are modest compared to economic crude oil resources at comparable prices, revenues from NGL production will enhance the economics of nonassociated gas projects.

27

Table 5. Volumes of oil, associated gas, and natural gas liquids (NGL) from undiscovered oil accumulations, estimated for the North Slope study area excluding resources in the 1002 Area of the Arctic National Wildlife Refuge, available as a function of specified market prices that offset costs of finding, developing, producing, and transporting the oil to market.

[Volumes represent the 95th-fractile, mean, and 5th-fractile estimates of undiscovered oil accumulations based on the North Slope study area aggregation except the 1002 Area has been excluded. Results of computations shown in the table are based on the assumption that sales of gas in gas discoveries are delayed 10 years. Prices are in 2007 dollars. Asc. gas, associated gas; $/bbl, dollars per barrel; BBO, billions of barrels of oil; TCF, trillions of cubic feet of gas; BBL, billions of barrels of natural gas liquids]

Oil price ($/bbl)	95th-fractile estimate			Mean estimate			5th-fractile estimate		
	Oil (BBO)	Asc. gas (TCF)	NGL (BBL)	Oil (BBO)	Asc. gas (TCF)	NGL (BBL)	Oil (BBO)	Asc. gas (TCF)	NGL (BBL)
27.00	0.00	0.00	0.00	0.00	0.00	0.00	0.00	0.00	0.00
30.00	0.00	0.00	0.00	0.66	0.75	0.01	0.88	0.64	0.01
33.00	1.70	1.92	0.03	2.40	2.67	0.05	3.08	2.38	0.03
36.00	2.30	2.58	0.05	3.05	3.42	0.06	3.91	3.14	0.05
39.00	2.80	3.15	0.06	4.17	4.70	0.09	5.65	4.64	0.08
42.00	4.00	4.23	0.07	5.87	6.66	0.12	7.69	6.46	0.10
45.00	5.15	5.18	0.08	6.90	7.80	0.14	9.61	8.26	0.14
48.00	6.41	6.19	0.08	8.06	9.08	0.17	10.47	9.09	0.15
51.00	6.69	6.48	0.09	8.62	9.71	0.18	11.32	9.94	0.17
54.00	7.13	6.82	0.09	9.39	10.59	0.20	11.95	10.49	0.18
57.00	7.70	7.33	0.10	9.82	11.08	0.21	12.52	11.01	0.19
60.00	7.89	7.54	0.10	10.10	11.40	0.21	13.19	11.69	0.20
63.00	8.36	7.96	0.10	10.65	12.02	0.23	13.46	11.93	0.21
66.00	8.43	8.02	0.10	10.92	12.33	0.23	13.79	12.22	0.21
69.00	8.84	8.40	0.11	11.04	12.46	0.24	13.97	12.38	0.22
72.00	9.03	8.59	0.11	11.28	12.73	0.24	14.20	12.63	0.22
75.00	9.12	8.68	0.11	11.41	12.88	0.24	14.54	12.92	0.23
78.00	9.34	8.85	0.11	11.59	13.07	0.25	14.70	13.03	0.23
81.00	9.36	8.87	0.11	11.62	13.09	0.25	14.79	13.12	0.23
84.00	9.50	9.00	0.11	11.80	13.28	0.25	14.88	13.19	0.23
87.00	9.59	9.06	0.11	12.01	13.48	0.26	15.07	13.35	0.23
90.00	9.70	9.17	0.12	12.02	13.50	0.26	15.14	13.42	0.23
93.00	9.72	9.18	0.12	12.12	13.60	0.26	15.25	13.51	0.24
96.00	9.80	9.24	0.12	12.20	13.67	0.26	15.30	13.54	0.24
99.00	9.93	9.33	0.12	12.23	13.71	0.26	15.35	13.58	0.24
102.00	9.94	9.33	0.12	12.27	13.74	0.26	15.43	13.62	0.24
105.00	9.95	9.34	0.12	12.29	13.76	0.26	15.48	13.65	0.24
108.00	9.96	9.34	0.12	12.29	13.76	0.26	15.56	13.74	0.24
111.00	10.01	9.40	0.12	12.34	13.79	0.26	15.61	13.78	0.24
114.00	10.07	9.44	0.12	12.38	13.84	0.26	15.61	13.79	0.24
117.00	10.12	9.47	0.12	12.49	13.94	0.26	15.62	13.79	0.24
120.00	10.19	9.53	0.12	12.53	13.99	0.26	15.69	13.84	0.24
123.00	10.19	9.53	0.12	12.54	13.99	0.26	15.69	13.85	0.24
126.00	10.19	9.53	0.12	12.54	13.99	0.26	15.75	13.88	0.24
129.00	10.19	9.53	0.12	12.54	13.99	0.26	15.77	13.89	0.24
132.00	10.25	9.57	0.12	12.54	14.00	0.27	15.81	13.92	0.24

Table 5. Volumes of oil, associated gas, and natural gas liquids (NGL) from undiscovered oil accumulations, estimated for the North Slope study area excluding resources in the 1002 Area of the Arctic National Wildlife Refuge, available as a function of specified market prices that offset costs of finding, developing, producing, and transporting the oil to market.—Continued

[Volumes represent the 95th-fractile, mean, and 5th-fractile estimates of undiscovered oil accumulations based on the North Slope study area aggregation except the 1002 Area has been excluded. Results of computations shown in the table are based on the assumption that sales of gas in gas discoveries are delayed 10 years. Prices are in 2007 dollars. Asc. gas, associated gas; $/bbl, dollars per barrel; BBO, billions of barrels of oil; TCF, trillions of cubic feet of gas; BBL, billions of barrels of natural gas liquids]

Oil price ($/bbl)	95th-fractile estimate			Mean estimate			5th-fractile estimate		
	Oil (BBO)	Asc. gas (TCF)	NGL (BBL)	Oil (BBO)	Asc. gas (TCF)	NGL (BBL)	Oil (BBO)	Asc. gas (TCF)	NGL (BBL)
135.00	10.25	9.57	0.12	12.59	14.04	0.27	15.88	13.98	0.24
138.00	10.29	9.61	0.12	12.66	14.10	0.27	15.88	13.98	0.24
141.00	10.29	9.61	0.12	12.67	14.11	0.27	15.88	13.99	0.24
144.00	10.39	9.69	0.12	12.70	14.14	0.27	15.89	13.99	0.24
147.00	10.39	9.69	0.12	12.73	14.16	0.27	15.92	14.01	0.24
150.00	10.44	9.73	0.12	12.76	14.19	0.27	15.95	14.03	0.24

Table 6. Volumes of nonassociated gas and natural gas liquids (NGL) from undiscovered gas accumulations, estimated for the entire North Slope study area, available as a function of specified market prices that offset costs of finding, developing, producing, and transporting the gas to market.

[Volumes represent the 95th-fractile, mean, and 5th-fractile estimates of gas accumulations based on the North Slope study area aggregation consisting of all State, Federal, and Native lands in the National Petroleum Reserve in Alaska (NPRA), the central North Slope, the 1002 Area, and the western North Slope. Results of computations shown in the table are based on the assumption that sales of gas in gas discoveries are delayed 10 and 20 years. Prices are in 2007 dollars; $/bbl, dollars per barrel; $/MCF, dollars per thousand cubic feet; TCF, trillions of cubic feet of gas; BBL, billions of barrels of natural gas liquids]

Oil price ($/bbl)	Gas price ($/MCF)	95th-fractile estimate				Mean estimate				5th-fractile estimate			
		10-year delay		20-year delay		10-year delay		20-year delay		10-year delay		20-year delay	
		Gas (TCF)	NGL (BBL)	Gas (TCF)	NGL (BBL)	Gas (TCF)	NGL (BBL)	Gas (TCF)	NGL (BBL)	Gas (TCF)	NGL (BBL)	Gas (TCF)	NGL (BBL)
27	3.00	0.00	0.00	0.00	0.00	0.00	0.00	0.00	0.00	0.00	0.00	0.00	0.00
30	3.33	0.00	0.00	0.00	0.00	0.00	0.00	0.00	0.00	0.00	0.00	0.00	0.00
33	3.67	0.00	0.00	0.00	0.00	0.00	0.00	0.00	0.00	0.00	0.00	0.00	0.00
36	4.00	0.00	0.00	0.00	0.00	0.00	0.00	0.00	0.00	0.00	0.00	0.00	0.00
39	4.33	0.00	0.00	0.00	0.00	0.00	0.00	0.00	0.00	0.00	0.00	0.00	0.00
42	4.67	0.00	0.00	0.00	0.00	0.00	0.00	0.00	0.00	0.00	0.00	0.00	0.00
45	5.00	0.00	0.00	0.00	0.00	0.00	0.00	0.00	0.00	0.00	0.00	0.00	0.00
48	5.33	0.00	0.00	0.00	0.00	0.00	0.00	0.00	0.00	0.00	0.00	0.00	0.00
51	5.67	0.00	0.00	0.00	0.00	0.00	0.00	0.00	0.00	0.00	0.00	0.00	0.00
54	6.00	0.37	0.04	0.37	0.04	0.65	0.05	0.57	0.05	0.99	0.07	0.98	0.07
57	6.33	0.66	0.05	0.66	0.05	1.70	0.08	1.08	0.07	2.71	0.09	2.70	0.09
60	6.67	1.37	0.06	1.37	0.06	3.04	0.09	2.52	0.09	5.10	0.12	5.09	0.12
63	7.00	2.00	0.07	1.91	0.07	6.14	0 13	5.58	0.13	12.70	0.20	12.68	0.20
66	7.33	6.42	0.20	5.50	0.19	9.67	0 18	9.07	0.17	17.89	0.26	17.87	0.26
69	7.67	7.28	0.21	7.30	0.21	12.03	0 21	11.41	0.21	20.12	0.28	20.10	0.28
72	8.00	10.78	0.26	10.77	0.25	16.83	0 27	14.36	0.25	31.94	0.40	23.58	0.32
75	8.33	15.59	0.31	15.57	0.31	20.67	0 32	19.96	0.31	41.06	0.51	33.59	0.43
78	8.67	18.47	0.34	17.33	0.33	26.79	0 39	22.12	0.34	47.14	0.57	35.88	0.46
81	9.00	21.47	0.37	19.66	0.35	29.01	0.42	24.31	0.36	59.12	0.69	46.83	0.57
84	9.33	26.95	0.43	23.81	0.39	38.36	0 53	26.50	0.39	64.20	0.74	52.11	0.62
87	9.67	29.45	0.46	26.28	0.42	45.17	0.61	30.29	0.44	69.83	0.79	55.53	0.66
90	10.00	30.71	0.47	26.47	0.43	45.77	0.61	36.35	0.50	74.59	0.84	62.01	0.72
93	10.33	33.83	0.51	27.52	0.44	49.69	0.66	37.77	0.52	77.31	0.86	63.85	0.74
96	10.67	37.70	0.54	33.64	0.50	54.97	0.72	39.65	0.54	81.16	0.90	66.61	0.77
99	11.00	40.06	0.57	34.63	0.51	58.07	0.75	40.06	0.54	87.48	0.95	71.37	0.81
102	11.33	40.15	0.57	34.72	0.51	59.45	0.77	41.07	0.55	90.89	0.99	72.02	0.82
105	11.67	40.59	0.57	34.72	0.51	62.24	0.80	41.51	0.56	90.89	0.99	72.02	0.82
108	12.00	40.73	0.58	34.86	0.51	62.35	0.80	45.34	0.60	91.10	1.00	74.90	0.85
111	12.33	41.06	0.58	34.86	0.51	65.35	0.83	45.37	0.60	91.54	1.00	76.64	0.86
114	12.67	42.54	0.60	34.86	0.51	65.91	0.84	45.37	0.60	96.27	1.05	76.75	0.87
117	13.00	42.57	0.60	34.90	0.51	67.68	0.86	45.41	0.60	96.30	1.05	77.53	0.88
120	13.33	44.23	0.62	35.33	0.52	69.79	0.88	45.41	0.60	98.43	1.06	77.53	0.88
123	13.67	46.32	0.63	36.58	0.53	69.79	0.88	47.51	0.62	100.80	1.09	77.53	0.88
126	14.00	46.32	0.63	36.90	0.54	69.79	0.88	47.51	0.62	102.35	1.10	80.23	0.90
129	14.33	46.37	0.64	36.90	0.54	69.79	0.88	47.52	0.62	102.56	1.10	81.05	0.90

Table 6. Volumes of nonassociated gas and natural gas liquids (NGL) from undiscovered gas accumulations, estimated for the entire North Slope study area, available as a function of specified market prices that offset costs of finding, developing, producing, and transporting the gas to market.—Continued

[Volumes represent the 95th-fractile, mean, and 5th-fractile estimates of gas accumulations based on the North Slope study area aggregation consisting of all State, Federal, and Native lands in the National Petroleum Reserve in Alaska (NPRA), the central North Slope, the 1002 Area, and the western North Slope. Results of computations shown in the table are based on the assumption that sales of gas in gas discoveries are delayed 10 and 20 years. Prices are in 2007 dollars; $/bbl, dollars per barrel; $/MCF, dollars per thousand cubic feet; TCF, trillions of cubic feet of gas; BBL, billions of barrels of natural gas liquids]

| Oil price ($/bbl) | Gas price ($/MCF) | 95th-fractile estimate | | | | Mean estimate | | | | 5th-fractile estimate | | | |
| | | 10-year delay | | 20-year delay | | 10-year delay | | 20-year delay | | 10-year delay | | 20-year delay | |
		Gas (TCF)	NGL (BBL)	Gas (TCF)	NGL (BBL)	Gas (TCF)	NGL (BBL)	Gas (TCF)	NGL (BBL)	Gas (TCF)	NGL (BBL)	Gas (TCF)	NGL (BBL)
132	14.67	46.37	0.64	38.93	0.56	69.79	0.88	47.52	0.62	102.57	1.10	81.06	0.90
135	15.00	46.53	0.64	38.93	0.56	71.80	0 91	47.85	0.63	103.70	1.11	83.20	0.92
138	15.33	47.37	0.65	38.94	0.56	74.05	0 93	49.72	0.64	104.62	1.12	86.72	0.96
141	15.67	47.37	0.65	38.94	0.56	75.29	0 94	53.42	0.69	105.72	1.13	86.72	0.96
144	16.00	47.37	0.65	39.00	0.56	75.69	0 95	55.89	0.71	106.12	1.13	88.55	0.98
147	16.33	48.55	0.66	41.27	0.58	75.75	0 95	55.89	0.71	106.92	1.14	88.55	0.98
150	16.67	50.38	0.68	41.27	0.58	76.29	0 95	55.89	0.71	106.92	1.14	88.55	0.98

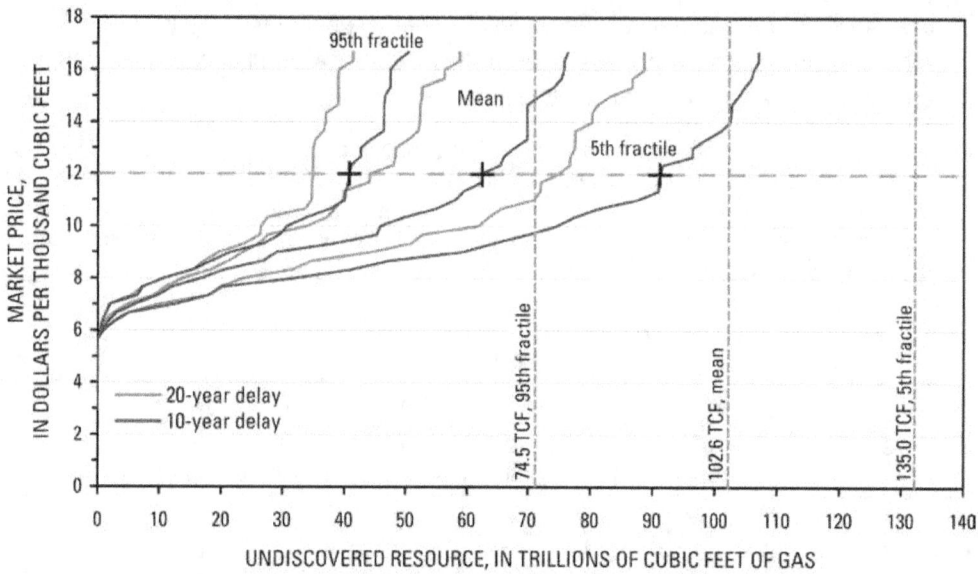

Figure 6. Summary graph of undiscovered economic nonassociated gas resources in the Alaska North Slope study area. The economic analysis assumed that gas is valued (in 2007 U.S. dollars) at two-thirds the value of oil, and the present value of gas was discounted for delays in pipeline availability of 10 years (blue curves) and 20 years (red curves); the green dashed vertical bars represent volumes of technically recoverable gas, providing upper limits to the volume of economically recoverable gas. Thus, at a market price of $12 per thousand cubic feet (orange dashed horizontal line) with a 10-year delay in pipeline availability, at the 95th-fractile resource estimate representing a 95 percent occurrence probability of at least 74.5 trillion cubic feet (TCF) of gas, 40.7 TCF is economic. Similarly, at the 5th-fractile estimate representing a 5 percent occurrence probability of at least 135.0 TCF of gas, 91.1 TCF is economic; at the mean estimate of 102.6 TCF of gas, 62.4 TCF is economic (see table 6.)

The cost functions show that nonassociated gas is responsive to market prices between $8/MCF and $12/MCF. At $8/MCF, only 15 to 24 percent of the technically recoverable gas can be found, developed, and produced commercially. However, at $12/MCF, the percentage of the economic technically recoverable gas jumps from 55 to 67 percent. The 50 percent increase in price results in an increase in the amount of economic gas at the 95th-fractile estimate from 10.8 to 40.7 and at the 5th-fractile estimate, economic gas increases from 31.9 TCF to 91.1 TCF.

Conclusions and Limitations

The North Slope study area contains several of the largest onshore discoveries in North America. Results of the geologic assessment confirm that the largest oil accumulations have already been found. The geologic assessment predicts size frequency distributions of undiscovered oil accumulations outside the 1002 Area to be marginal in size (less than 500 MMBO; 3 TCF). Many of these marginally sized accumulations may not be economic unless they occur in clusters and can share transportation facilities. TAPS has been in operation for more than 30 years, and declining flow rates jeopardize its continuing operation. The timely exploration and development of new oil fields are particularly important to their commercial viability before TAPS is abandoned. In contrast to the oil resource development, natural gas resources have been stranded on the North Slope for decades and the timing of construction of the gas transportation system is uncertain.

The surge and volatility in international oil prices from mid-2005 through 2008 have produced chaotic market conditions for the oil and gas industry service sector. Costs have escalated with price increases and have appeared to dampen new exploration and development. However, as prices increase, the unforeseen opportunities for new development technology and innovative development strategies will undoubtedly occur. The geologic assessments were based on historical oil and gas recovery factors assuming standard primary and waterflood development practices. If high oil prices are sustained into the future, it is expected that new technology and development strategies will lead to higher recovery factors. These factors would increase both the technically and economically recoverable resource estimates from the current assessment.

The dampening effect of an additional 10-year delay tends to reduce payoff and results in a reduction of 14 to 27 percent in the amount of economic gas that can be found and discovered at market prices of $12/MCF. At $12/MCF, the volume associated with the reduction in the economic gas based on the mean estimate is significant (17.0 TCF) relative to the proven gas reserves in the area (30 to 33 TCF). This effect on gas economics also affects the expected profitability of oil exploration where oil and gas accumulations are thought to occur in the same area.

Acknowledgments

We are grateful for the reviews of Keith Long, Ken Bird, and James Coleman of the U.S. Geological Survey and James Craig of the Minerals Management Service. We also would like to thank Elizabeth Good (USGS) for editorial assistance and Anna Glover (USGS) and Cathy Knutson (USGS) for graphic design support.

References Cited

Alaska Department of Revenue, Tax Division, 2007, Fall 2007 revenue sources book: Anchorage, Alaska, 126 p. (Also available online at
http://www.tax.alaska.gov/programs/documentviewer/viewer.aspx?255.)

Alaska Department of Revenue, Tax Division, 2008, Spring 2008 forecast: Anchorage, Alaska, 11 p., available online at http://www.tax.alaska.gov/programs/documentviewer/viewer.aspx?1338f. (Accessed August 2008.)

American Petroleum Institute, 1997–2005, Joint association survey of drilling costs: Washington, D.C., American Petroleum Institute, pagination varies by year.

ARCO Alaska Inc., Anadarko Petroleum Corp., and Union Texas Petroleum LLC, 1998, Alpine written testimony, Alpine Pool Rules Hearing, Alaska Oil and Gas Conservation Commission, December 3, 1998: Anchorage, Alaska.

Atkinson, Ian, Theuveny, Bertrand, Berard, Michel, Conort, Gilbert, Groves, Joel, Lowe, Trey, McDiarmid, Allan, Mehdizadeh, Parviz, Perciot, Patrick, Pinguet, Bruno, Smith, Gerald, and Williamson, K.J., 2005, A new horizon in multiphase flow measurement: Oilfield Review, v. 16, no. 14, Winter 2004/2005, p. 52–63. (Also available online at
http://www.slb.com/media/services/resources/oilfieldreview/ors04/win04/05_multiphase_flow.pdf.)

Attanasi, E.D., 1998, Economics and the 1995 National Assessment of United States Oil and Gas Resources: U.S. Geological Survey Circular 1145, 35 p. (Also available at
http://pubs.usgs.gov/circ/1998/c1145/c1145.html.)

Attanasi, E.D., 1999, Economics of undiscovered oil in the 1002 Area of the Arctic National Wildlife Refuge, chap. EA *of* ANWR Assessment Team, The oil and gas resource potential of the Arctic National Wildlife Refuge 1002 Area, Alaska: U.S. Geological Survey Open-File Report 98–34, 59 p., on CD-ROM. (Also available online at *http://pubs.usgs.gov/of/1998/ofr-98-0034/.*) (Accessed February 27, 2009.)

Attanasi, E.D., 2003, Economics of undiscovered oil in Federal lands on the National Petroleum Reserve, Alaska: U.S. Geological Survey Open-File Report 03–44, 63 p., available only online at *http://pubs.usgs.gov/of/2003/of03-044/.* (Accessed February 27, 2009.)

Attanasi, E.D., 2005a, Undiscovered oil resources in the Federal portion of the 1002 Area of the Arctic National Wildlife Refuge—An economic update: U.S. Geological Survey Open-File Report 2005–1217, 29 p., available only online at *http://pubs.usgs.gov/of/2005/1217/.* (Accessed February 27, 2009.)

Attanasi, E.D., 2005b, Economics of 1998 U.S. Geological Survey's 1002 Area regional assessment— An economic update: U.S. Geological Survey Open-File Report 2005–1359, 10 p., available only online at *http://pubs.usgs.gov/of/2005/1359/.* (Accessed February 27, 2009.)

Attanasi, E.D., and Bird, K.J. [1996], Economics and undiscovered conventional oil and gas accumulations in the 1995 National Assessment of U.S. Oil and Gas Resources—Alaska: U.S. Geological Survey Open-File Report 95–75–J, 48 p., available online at *http://pubs.er.usgs.gov/usgspubs/ofr/ofr9575J.* (Accessed February 27, 2009.)

Attanasi, E.D., and Freeman, P.A., 2005, Economics of undiscovered oil and gas in the central North Slope, Alaska: U.S. Geological Survey Open-File Report 2005–1276, 39 p. (Version 1.1 was released January 13, 2006, and is available online at *http://pubs.usgs.gov/of/2005/1276/.*) (Accessed February 27, 2009.)

Baker, R.A., Gehman, H.M., James, W.R., and White, D.A., 1984, Geologic field number and size assessments of oil and gas plays: American Association of Petroleum Geologists Bulletin, v. 68, no. 4, p. 426–432.

Bird, K.J., 1999, Assessment overview, chap. AO *of* ANWR Assessment Team, The oil and gas resource potential of the Arctic National Wildlife Refuge 1002 Area, Alaska: U.S. Geological Survey Open-File Report 98–34, 56 p., on CD-ROM. (Also available online at *http://pubs.usgs.gov/of/1998/ofr-98-0034/.*) (Accessed February 27, 2009.)

Bird, K.J., and Houseknecht, D.W., 2002, U.S. Geological Survey 2002 petroleum resource assessment of the National Petroleum Reserve in Alaska (NPRA): U.S. Geological Survey Fact Sheet 045–02, 6 p., available online at *http://pubs.usgs.gov/fs/2002/fs045-02/.* (Accessed February 27, 2009.)

British Petroleum Exploration (Alaska), 1996, Northstar Development Project—Conceptual Engineering Report, report submitted for evaluation to the Alaska Department of Natural Resources: Anchorage, Alaska

ConocoPhillips, 2007, ANS natural gas pipeline—Proposal to the State of Alaska, November 30, 2007: [Houston,] ConocoPhillips, 115 p. (Available from the Alaska Department of Natural Resources, Anchorage, Alaska.)

Corbett, K.T., Bowen, R.R., and Petersen, C.W., 2003, High strength steel pipeline economics, *in* v. 4 *of* Ayer, Raghavan, Langen, Ivar, Knapp, R.H., and Chung, J.S., eds., Proceedings of the Thirteenth International Offshore and Polar Engineering Conference, 25–30th May 2003, Honolulu, Hawaii: Cupertino, Calif., International Society of Offshore and Polar Engineers, p. 105–112.

Craig, J.D., 2002, Economic analysis of the development alternatives for the Liberty prospect, Beaufort Sea, Alaska, app. D–1 *in* v. IV, Appendices, *of* Liberty development and production plan; Final environmental impact statement: Minerals Management Service [Report] OCS EIS/EA 2002–019, p.

D1–1 to D1–22, available online at
http://www.mms.gov/alaska/ref/EIS%20EA/libertyfeis/Documents/Liberty%20FEIS%20Vol%204.pdf.
(Accessed April 8, 2009.)

Energy Information Administration, 2008, Annual energy outlook 2008, with projections to 2030: Energy Information Administration [Report] DOE/EIA–0383(2008), 215 p., available online at *http://www.eia.doe.gov/oiaf/aeo/pdf/0383(2008).pdf.* (Accessed April 8, 2009.)

Garrity, C.P., Houseknecht, D.W., and Bird, K.J., 2002, U.S. Geological Survey 2002 petroleum resource assessment of the National Petroleum Reserve in Alaska (NPRA)—GIS play maps: U.S. Geological Survey Open-File Report 02–439, available only online at *http://pubs.usgs.gov/of/2002/of02-439/.* (Accessed February 27, 2009.)

Garrity, C.P., Houseknecht, D.W., Bird, K.J., Potter, C.J., Moore, T.E., Nelson, P.H., and Schenk, C.J., 2005, U.S. Geological Survey 2005 oil and gas resource assessment of the central North Slope, Alaska; Play maps and results: U.S. Geological Survey Open-File Report 2005–1182, 24 p., available online at *http://pubs.usgs.gov/of/2005/1182/.* (Accessed February 27, 2009.)

Gingrich, Dean, Knock, Doug, and Masters, Ron, 2001, Geophysical interpretation methods applied at Alpine oil field, North Slope Alaska: The Leading Edge, v. 20, no. 7 (July), p. 730–738.

Houseknecht, D.W., and Bird, K.J., 2006, Oil and gas resources of the Arctic Alaska Petroleum Province, chap. A *of* Haeussler, P.J., and Galloway, J.P., eds., Studies by the U.S. Geological Survey in Alaska, 2005: U.S. Geological Survey Professional Paper 1732, p. 1–11, available only online at *http://pubs.usgs.gov/pp/pp1732/pp1732a/index.html.* (Accessed February 27, 2009.)

IHS Inc., 2007, QUE$TOR petroleum field development and production cost database, v. 9.5: Englewood, Colo., IHS Inc.

Joshi, S.D., 1991a, Drainage areas and well spacing, *in* Fritz, R.D., Horn, M.K., and Joshi, S.D., eds., Geological aspects of horizontal drilling: American Association of Petroleum Geologists Continuing Education Course Note Series 33, p. 65–78.

Joshi, S.D., 1991b, Factor influencing productivity, *in* Fritz, R.D., Horn, M.K., and Joshi, S.D., eds., Geological aspects of horizontal drilling: American Association of Petroleum Geologists Continuing Education Course Note Series 33, p. 80–90.

Kaltenbach, Bob, Walsh, Chantal, Foerster, Cathy, Walsh, Tom, MacDonald, Jan, Stokes, Pete, Livesey, Chris, and Nebesky, Will, 2004, North Slope of Alaska facility sharing study, prepared for Division of Oil and Gas, Alaska Department of Natural Resources, by Petrotechnical Resources of Alaska: 62 p., available online at
http://www.dog.dnr.state.ak.us/oil/products/publications/otherreports/nsfacility/share.htm. (Accessed February 27, 2009.)

Kuuskraa, V.A., Morra, F., Jr., and Godec, M.L., 1987, Importance of cost/price relationships for least-cost oil and gas resources, *in* Proceedings of 1987 Hydrocarbon Economics and Evaluation Symposium, Dallas, Texas: Richardson, Tex., Society of Petroleum Engineers, SPE Paper 16290, p. 25–42.

National Petroleum Council, 1981a, U.S. Arctic oil and gas: Washington D.C., National Petroleum Council, December 1981, 286 p.

National Petroleum Council, 1981b, Working papers of the Production Task Group of the National Petroleum Council's Committee on Arctic Oil and Gas Resources: Washington, D.C., National Petroleum Council, 372 p.

National Petroleum Council, 2003, Balancing natural gas policy—Fueling the demands of a growing economy, v. IV, Supply Task Force Report: Washington, D.C., National Petroleum Council, 456 p.

Nehring Associates, Inc., 2004, Significant oil and gas fields of the United States database: Colorado Springs, Colo., Nehring Associates, Inc.

Nelson, Kristen, 2004, Alternatives to Alpine satellite project proposed: Anchorage, Alaska, Petroleum News, January 28, 2004, p. 1, 12–13.

Redman, R.S., 2002, Horizontal miscible water alternating gas development of the Alpine field, Alaska, *in* Society of Petroleum Engineers Western Regional/AAPG Pacific Section Joint Meeting, 20–22nd May 2002, Anchorage, Alaska: Richardson, Tex., Society of Petroleum Engineers, SPE Paper 76819, 8 p.

Schuenemeyer, J.H., 1999, Methodology, chap. ME *of* ANWR Assessment Team, The oil and gas resource potential of the Arctic National Wildlife Refuge 1002 Area, Alaska: U.S. Geological Survey Open-File Report 98–34, 28 p., on CD-ROM. (Also available online at *http://pubs.usgs.gov/of/1998/ofr-98-0034/*.) (Accessed February 27, 2009.)

Schuenemeyer, J.H., 2003, Methodology and results for the assessment of oil and gas resources, National Petroleum Reserve, Alaska: U.S. Geological Survey Open-File Report 03–118, 201 p., available online at *http://geopubs.wr.usgs.gov/open-file/of03-118/*. (Accessed February 27, 2009.)

Schuenemeyer, J.H., 2005, Methodology for the 2005 USGS assessment of undiscovered oil and gas resources, central North Slope, Alaska: U.S. Geological Survey Open-File Report 2005–1410, 82 p., available online at *http://pubs.usgs.gov/of/2005/1410/*. (Accessed February 27, 2009.)

Thomas, C.P., Doughty, T.C., Faulder, D.D., Harrision, W.E., Irving, J.S., Jamison, H.C., and White, G.J., 1991, Alaska oil and gas energy wealth or vanishing opportunity: Idaho Falls, Idaho, E.G. and G, Idaho, Inc., DOE/ID/01570-H1, 279 p.

Thomas, C.P., Faulder, D.D., Doughty, T.C., Hite, D.M., and White, G.J., 2007, Alaska North Slope oil and gas—A promising future or an area in decline? (full report): National Energy Technology Laboratory [Report] DOE/ NETL-2007/1279, 479 p., available online at *http://www.netl.doe.gov/technologies/oil-gas/publications/EPreports/ANSFullReportFinalAugust2007.pdf*. (Accessed April 9, 2009.)

TransCanada, 2007, Application for license—Alaska Gasline Inducement Act, Public application and appendices: Calgary, Alberta, Canada, TransCanada Pipelines Limited, available online at *http://www.gov.state.ak.us/agia/*. (Accessed September 30, 2008.)

Vidas, E.H., Hugman, R.H., and Haverkamp, D.S., 1993, Guide to the hydrocarbon supply model—1993 update: Arlington, Va., Energy and Environmental Analysis, Inc., prepared for the Gas Research Institute, 272 p.

Young, J.H., and Hauser, W.S., 1986, Economics of oil and gas production from the Arctic Refuge (ANWR): Anchorage, Alaska, U.S. Bureau of Land Management, Alaska State Office, 101 p.

Appendix 1. Volumes Associated with the Mean Estimate for Each Play in Each of the Four Assessment Areas

Tables A1-1 through A1-4 provide the volumes of undiscovered oil and gas resources associated with the mean estimates of each play assessed in the National Petroleum Reserve in Alaska (NPRA), the central North Slope, the 1002 Area of the Arctic National Wildlife Refuge and the western North Slope subareas (see text fig. 1). The original assessment data from the earlier assessments of the 1002 Area (Bird, 1999), the NPRA (Bird and Houseknecht, 2002), and the central North Slope (Garrity and others, 2005) were adjusted by the assessment geologists to reflect a common minimum size accumulation with separate distributions for numbers of oil and gas prospects. These data were probabilistically aggregated along with the assessment results for the western North Slope to arrive at the volumes shown in table 1 of the text (written communications, J.H. Schuenemeyer, Southwest Statistical Consulting, November 2007). Text figures 2*A* and 2*B* show the aggregate accumulation frequency size distributions associated with the 95th- and 5th-fractile estimates as well as the mean value estimates.

Table A1–1.   Mean estimates of undiscovered technically recoverable volumes of conventional oil and gas by play for the National Petroleum Reserve in Alaska.

[Asc. gas, associated gas; Nonasc. gas, nonassociated gas; BBO, billions of barrels of oil; TCF, trillions of cubic feet of gas; BBL, billions of barrels of natural gas liquids (NGL); -- (dashes), volume smaller than the minimum assessed accumulation size]

Play	Oil accumulations			Gas accumulations	
	Oil (BBO)	Asc. gas (TCF)	NGL (BBL)	Nonasc. gas (TCF)	NGL (BBL)
Brookian Topset	0.22	0.19	0.00	0.19	0.00
Brookian Clinoform North	1.28	1.09	0.01	0.67	0.01
Brookian Clinoform Central	1.04	1.32	0.03	5.48	0.07
Brookian Clinoform South-Shallow	0.49	0.35	0.00	2.33	0.03
Brookian Clinoform South-Deep	--	--	--	3.98	0.05
Beaufortian Cretaceous Topset North	0.11	0.09	0.00	0.42	0.00
Beaufortian Cretaceous Topset South	--	--	--	2.20	0.03
Beaufortian Upper Jurassic Topset NE	4.96	6.05	0.11	--	--
Beaufortian Upper Jurassic Topset SE	0.00	0.00	0.00	5.30	0.07
Beaufortian Upper Jurassic Topset NW	1.93	2.34	0.04	--	--
Beaufortian Upper Jurassic Topset SW	--	--	--	5.43	0.07
Beaufortian Lower Jurassic Topset	0.09	0.05	0.00	0.79	0.01
Beaufortian Clinoform	0.01	0.00	0.00	0.80	0.01
Brookian Topset Structural	0.14	0.00	0.00	11.00	0.09
Torok Structural	0.03	0.02	0.00	18.83	0.17
Ellesmerian Structural	0.00	0.00	0.00	2.06	0.03
Ellesmerian Thrust Belt	0.01	0.01	0.00	1.48	0.02
Ellesmerian-Ivishak	0.10	0.06	0.00	0.11	0.00
Ellesmerian Echooka North	0.01	0.01	0.00	0.01	0.00
Ellesmerian Echooka South	--	--	--	0.50	0.01
Ellesmerian Lisburne North	0.03	0.02	0.00	0.02	0.00
Ellesmerian Lisburne South	--	--	--	0.65	0.01
Ellesmerian Endicott North	0.00	0.00	0.00	--	--
Ellesmerian Endicott South	--	--	--	1.08	0.01
Total	10.47	11.59	0.21	63.34	0.68

Table A1–2. Mean estimates of undiscovered technically recoverable volumes of conventional oil and gas by play for the central North Slope.

[Asc. gas; associated gas; Nonasc. gas, nonassociated gas; BBO, billions of barrels of oil; TCF, trillions of cubic feet of gas; BBL, billions of barrels of natural gas liquids (NGL); -- (dashes), volume smaller than the minimum assessed accumulation size]

Play	Oil accumulations			Gas accumulations	
	Oil (BBO)	Asc. gas (TCF)	NGL (BBL)	Nonasc. gas (TCF)	NGL (BBL)
Brookian Clinoform	1.48	1.66	0.03	4.86	0.06
Brookian Topset	0.34	0.25	0.00	0.18	0.00
Beaufortian Upper Jurassic Topset East	0.00	0.00	0.00	0.06	0.00
Beaufortian Upper Jurassic Topset West	0.12	0.11	0.00	0.12	0.00
Beaufortian Clinoform	0.09	0.13	0.00	0.43	0.01
Beaufortian Kuparuk Topset	0.09	0.07	0.00	0.18	0.00
Beaufortian Cretaceous Shelf Margin	--	--	--	0.35	0.00
Triassic Barrow Arch	0.35	0.43	0.01	0.00	0.00
Ivishak Barrow Flank	--	--	--	0.17	0.00
Endicott	--	--	--	0.13	0.00
Endicott Truncation	0.06	0.07	0.00	--	--
Franklinian	0.01	0.01	0.00	--	--
Lisburne Barrow Arch	0.09	0.09	0.00	--	--
Lisburne Barrow Flank	--	--	--	0.59	0.01
Kemik-Thompson	0.23	0.41	0.02	1.92	0.02
Basement Involved Structural	0.02	0.01	0.00	2.35	0.03
Beaufortian Structural	0.01	0.01	0.00	1.63	0.02
Brookian Clinoform Structural South	0.01	0.01	0.00	1.74	0.02
Brookian Clinoform Structural North	0.12	0.13	0.00	0.18	0.00
Brookian Topset Structural South	0.02	0.01	0.00	2.22	0.02
Brookian Topset Structural North	0.26	0.10	0.00	0.25	0.00
Thrust Belt Triangle Zone	0.05	0.03	0.00	3.47	0.04
Thrust Belt Lisburne	0.07	0.07	0.00	3.16	0.04
Ellesmerian Structural	--	--	--	1.11	0.01
Total	3.41	3.60	0.08	25.10	0.29

Table A1–3. Mean estimates of undiscovered technically recoverable volumes of conventional oil and gas by play for the 1002 Area of the Arctic National Wildlife Refuge.

[Asc. gas, associated gas; Nonasc. gas, nonassociated gas; BBO, billions of barrels of oil; TCF, trillions of cubic feet of gas; BBL, billions of barrels of natural gas liquids (NGL); -- (dashes), volume smaller than the minimum assessed accumulation size]

Play	Oil accumulations			Gas accumulations	
	Oil (BBO)	Asc. gas (TCF)	NGL (BBL)	Nonasc. gas (TCF)	NGL (BBL)
Topset	6.18	1.70	0.01	--	--
Tubidite	1.59	1.39	0.08	--	--
Wedge	0.50	0.26	0.01	--	--
Thompson	0.36	0.46	0.04	0.23	0.02
Kemik	0.05	0.06	0.01	0.06	0.00
Undeformed Franklinian	0.10	0.18	0.02	0.18	0.02
Thin-Skinned Thrust Belt	1.15	0.32	0.00	1.45	0.02
Ellesmerian Thrust Belt	--	--	--	0.87	0.02
Deformed Franklinian	0.05	0.04	0.00	0.82	0.04
Niquanak/Aurora	0.36	0.34	0.02	0.21	0.01
Total	10.35	4.76	0.19	3.81	0.13

Table A1–4. Mean estimates of undiscovered technically recoverable volumes of conventional oil and gas by play for the western North Slope.

[Asc. gas, associated gas; Nonasc. gas, nonassociated gas; BBO, billions of barrels of oil; TCF, trillions of cubic feet of gas; BBL, billions of barrels of natural gas liquids (NGL); -- (dashes), volume smaller than the minimum assessed accumulation size]

Play	Oil accumulations			Gas accumulations	
	Oil (BBO)	Asc. gas (TCF)	NGL (BBL)	Nonasc. gas (TCF)	NGL (BBL)
Brookian Clinoform	--	--	--	1.4312	0.0174
Brookian Topset	0.0059	0.0035	0.0000	0.4294	0.0035
Nanushuk Structural	0.0233	0.0105	0.0001	2.0571	0.012
Southwest Foothills Structural	0.0466	0.0323	0.0006	6.4434	0.0823
Total	0.0758	0.0463	0.0007	10.3611	0.1152

Appendix 2. Allocation of Play Resources to Economic Zones

The procedure for the allocation of play resources to economic zones begins with the published play boundaries for the central North Slope (Garrity and others, 2005), the National Petroleum Reserve in Alaska (NPRA) (Garrity and others, 2003), and the 1002 Area of the Arctic National Wildlife Refuge (ANWR) (Bird, 1999). The western North Slope subarea constituted a single economic zone. For some plays, the geologists provided supplemental information that enabled subdivision of plays between oil-prone and gas-prone areas. The economic zones encompassed onshore Native, Federal, and State lands and offshore State areas. Text figure 4 shows the individual economic zones. The economic zones are of a size that development hubs could evolve in each. The allocations of total play volumes by primary product (oil and nonassociated gas resources) were expressed as percentages. The same percentages were used to allocate resources at the 95th-fractile, the mean, and the 5th-fractile estimates. For an individual play, accumulation size class allocations were the same percentages as the primary product volume allocations. However, inasmuch as each economic zone has a different mix of plays, the size frequency distribution for undiscovered accumulations will be different across zones of the same study subarea.

The NPRA was divided into eight economic zones, and 24 plays were assessed. The assessors posited that oil accumulations were more likely to occur in the northern and eastern parts of the NPRA and that the southern and western parts of the NPRA would be more prospective for natural gas accumulations. Table A2-1 shows the percentage of total oil resources and the percentage of nonassociated natural gas resources allocated to each of the eight economic zones.

There were 24 plays delineated by the geologists for the central North Slope study subarea, which has 3 economic zones. Geologists posited that the northern portion of the area is oil prone and the southern portion is gas prone. Table A2-2 shows the percentage allocations of oil and gas for plays for this study subarea.

There were 10 plays delineated by geologists for the 1002 Area of the Arctic National Wildlife Refuge (ANWR), which has 2 economic zones (table A2-3). Plays in the western economic zone are characterized by a larger field size and are more oil prone than the plays in the eastern economic zone.

The western North Slope represented a single economic zone, and so the four plays delineated by the assessment geologists (see table A1-4) were not subdivided. The undiscovered accumulations assessed in the western North Slope were predominantly gas.

Table A2–1. Percentage allocations of oil in oil accumulations and gas in gas accumulations for plays of the National Petroleum Reserve in Alaska to economic zones N110, N120, N130, N210, N220, N230, N320, and N330, as identified in text figure 4.

Play	N110	N120	N130	N210	N220	N230	N320	N330
				Oil in oil accumulations				
Brookian Topset	22	23	20	15	10	10	0	0
Brookian Clinoform North	49	40	10	1	0	0	0	0
Brookian Clinoform Central	4	20	17	36	20	3	0	0
Brookian Clinoform South-Shallow	0	0	0	20	54	23	1	2
Brookian Clinoform South-Deep	0	0	0	0	0	0	0	0
Beaufortian Cretaceous Topset North	44	42	12	2	0	0	0	0
Beaufortian Cretaceous Topset South	0	0	0	0	0	0	0	0
Beaufortian Upper Jurassic Topset Northeast	58	40	0	2	0	0	0	0
Beaufortian Upper Jurassic Topset Southeast	0	0	0	0	0	0	0	0
Beaufortian Upper Jurassic Topset Northwest	0	20	80	0	0	0	0	0
Beaufortian Upper Jurassic Topset Southwest	0	0	0	0	0	0	0	0
Beaufortian Lower Jurassic Topset	10	55	35	0	0	0	0	0
Beaufortian Clinoform	100	0	0	0	0	0	0	0
Brookian Topset Structural	2	12	17	17	27	23	1	1
Torok Structural	1	3	7	14	28	45	1	1
Ellesmerian Structural	0	0	0	0	0	0	0	0
Thrust Belt	0	0	0	0	0	0	25	75
Ellesmerian Ivishak	45	32	20	1	1	1	0	0
Ellesmerian Echooka North	79	15	6	0	0	0	0	0
Ellesmerian Echooka South	0	0	0	0	0	0	0	0
Ellesmerian Lisburne North	75	25	0	0	0	0	0	0
Ellesmerian Lisburne South	0	0	0	0	0	0	0	0
Ellesmerian Endicott North	60	40	0	0	0	0	0	0
Ellesmerian Endicott South	0	0	0	0	0	0	0	0

Table A2-1. Percentage allocations of oil in oil accumulations and gas in gas accumulations for plays of the National Petroleum Reserve in Alaska to economic zones N110, N120, N130, N210, N220, N230, N320, and N330, as identified in text figure 4.—Continued

Play	N110	N120	N130	N210	N220	N230	N320	N330
Gas in gas accumulations								
Brookian Topset	7	13	19	12	21	28	0	0
Brookian Clinoform North	24	45	30	1	0	0	0	0
Brookian Clinoform Central	2	15	40	13	15	15	0	0
Brookian Clinoform South-Shallow	0	0	0	7	30	60	1	2
Brookian Clinoform South-Deep	0	0	0	7	30	60	1	2
Beaufortian Cretaceous Topset North	33	40	20	7	0	0	0	0
Beaufortian Cretaceous Topset South	0	8	35	15	30	12	0	0
Beaufortian Upper Jurassic Topset Northeast	0	0	0	0	0	0	0	0
Beaufortian Upper Jurassic Topset Southeast	3	15	0	35	47	0	0	0
Beaufortian Upper Jurassic Topset Northwest	0	0	0	0	0	0	0	0
Beaufortian Upper Jurassic Topset Southwest	0	5	60	0	15	20	0	0
Beaufortian Lower Jurassic Topset	0	25	45	0	10	20	0	0
Beaufortian Clinoform	100	0	0	0	0	0	0	0
Brookian Topset Structural	2	12	17	17	27	23	1	1
Torok Structural	1	3	7	12	24	40	4	9
Ellesmerian Structural	0	0	0	12	25	50	4	9
Thrust Belt	0	0	0	0	0	0	25	75
Ellesmerian Ivishak	45	32	20	1	1	1	0	0
Ellesmerian Echooka North	79	15	6	0	0	0	0	0
Ellesmerian Echooka South	0	15	40	25	10	10	0	0
Ellesmerian Lisburne North	75	25	0	0	0	0	0	0
Ellesmerian Lisburne South	0	20	30	25	20	5	0	0
Ellesmerian Endicott North	60	40	0	0	0	0	0	0
Ellesmerian Endicott South	20	20	20	20	15	5	0	0

Table A2–2. Percentage allocations of oil in oil accumulations and gas in gas accumulations for plays of the central North Slope to economic zones C110, C120, and C130, as identified in text figure 4.

Play	Oil in oil accumulations			Gas in gas accumulations		
	C110	C120	C130	C110	C120	C130
Brookian Clinoform	53	48	0	0	56	44
Brookian Topset	46	54	0	0	62	38
Beaufortian Upper Jurassic Topset East	5	95	0	0	100	0
Beaufortian Upper Jurassic Topset West	91	9	0	0	100	0
Beaufortian Clinoform	45	56	0	0	100	0
Beaufortian Kuparuk Topset	71	29	0	0	100	0
Beaufortian Cretaceous Shelf Margin	0	100	0	0	100	0
Triassic Barrow Arch	100	0	0	100	0	0
Ivishak Barrow Flank	6	94	0	6	94	0
Endicott	39	61	0	39	61	0
Endicott Truncation	100	0	0	100	0	0
Franklinian	100	0	0	100	0	0
Lisburne Barrow Arch	73	27	0	73	27	0
Lisburne Barrow Flank	3	97	0	3	97	0
Kemik-Thompson	60	40	0	0	100	0
Basement Involved Structural	0	72	29	0	72	29
Beaufortian Structural	0	82	18	0	82	18
Brookian Clinoform Structural South	0	79	21	0	79	21
Brookian Clinoform Structural North	0	100	0	0	100	0
Brookian Topset Structural South	0	72	28	0	72	28
Brookian Topset Structural North	0	100	0	0	100	0
Thrust Belt Triangle Zone	0	9	91	0	9	91
Thrust Belt Lisburne	0	0	100	0	0	100
Ellesmerian Structural	0	47	53	0	47	53

Table A2–3. Percentage allocations of oil in oil accumulations and gas in gas accumulations for plays of the 1002 Area of the Arctic National Wildlife Refuge to economic zones A110 and A120, as identified in text figure 4.

Play	Oil in oil accumulations		Gas in gas accumulations	
	A110	A120	A110	A120
Topset	86	14	0	0
Turbidite	95	5	0	0
Wedge	100	0	100	0
Thompson	100	0	100	0
Kemik	100	0	100	0
Undeformed Franklinian	100	0	100	0
Thin-Skinned Thrust Belt	25	75	25	75
Ellesmerian Thrust Belt	0	0	10	90
Deformed Franklinian	90	10	90	10
Niguanak/Aurora	0	100	0	100

Appendix 3. Documentation of Cost Estimates

Transportation Costs

The text discussion explains the rationale for the assumptions relating to the dominant cost transportation component, that is, the cost component from North Slope collection points, either Pump Station 1 or the proposed gas conditioning plant, to the respective market. To review, the assumed Trans-Alaska Pipeline System (TAPS) tariff is $4.87 per barrel from Pump Station 1 to Valdez. In addition to this cost, there is a cost of $1.61 per barrel to transport oil from Valdez to the market. There is an estimated cost of $4.42 per thousand cubic feet ($4.42/MCF) for natural gas conditioning and pipeline shipment to the U.S. Midwest market.

The assessment results implied that likely discovery sizes are expected to be modest by Arctic standards (less than 500 MMBO and 3 TCF). At the mean estimate, the technically recoverable resources are expected to be contained in 179 oil and 145 nonassociated gas accumulations. The economic zones provide a basis for transportation cost sharing of overland pipelines from the economic zone to TAPS or the proposed gas conditioning plant. Tables A2-1, A2-2, and A2-3 list the play allocations of oil and nonassociated gas accumulations to the economic zones within each North Slope subarea. Individual discoveries are required to bear the full cost of construction and operation of the feeder pipeline from the field to the overland regional pipeline. These pipeline costs are recovered by a tariff charged by the feeder pipeline owner. Both feeder and regional pipelines are operated as common carriers.

Feeder and Regional Pipeline Assumptions

A hypothetical transportation system moves oil and gas to the central North Slope subarea where TAPS and a proposed natural gas conditioning plant are located. This system consists of feeder lines from the fields to a regional pipeline. For each discovery size class, the peak or plateau annual production volume was computed for the representative oil and gas discovery. The required diameter for the feeder lines from individual discoveries to the regional pipeline was calculated to accommodate the peak or plateau flow rates. The investment costs of the individual feeder lines depend on the pipeline's diameter and length, that is, the average distance from the field to a regional pipeline. The tariff[19] or charge for transporting the oil from the outlying discovery to a regional pipeline hub was computed as if the feeder pipeline were operated as a regulated common carrier and permitted a 12 percent after-tax rate of return on investment cost. The calculated tariff includes the after-tax rate of return, operating costs, taxes, and recovery of the initial investment during the nominal life of the field.

The size of the crude oil or gas product pipeline from the field to the regional pipeline was calculated such that its capacity (regulated by its diameter) would be sufficient to move the discovery's peak annual plateau production to the regional line. The oil and conventional gas pipeline cost data were generated with the QUE$TOR software (IHS Inc., 2007). The investment costs were estimated and expressed in dollars per inch-diameter per mile. The costs include the installed pipe, the right of way, and the initial pump system. The base cost is $163,000 per inch-diameter per mile for crude oil and $175,000 per inch-diameter per mile for a conventional gas line.

Base costs were scaled up to include all pipelines bundled together and installed in the overland pipeline corridor. To estimate costs of these additions for all feeder lines and in some cases for the

---

[19]The term "tariff," as used in this report, is the charge by a publicly regulated entity; in this case a regulated common carrier.

regional oil pipelines, diameters were increased to account for the additional bundling of utility lines and seawater lines (for waterflood of oil discoveries)[20] to the operating field. These lines may use the same vertical support members and right of way as the pipeline transporting produced oil and gas to the regional pipeline. To account for this extra cost, the initial investment cost per inch-diameter per mile was increased by 100 percent for oil accumulations requiring import of injection water and 50 percent per inch-diameter per mile for gas discoveries.

Booster pump stations were added to the oil and natural gas pipelines at intervals of 100 miles from the source. Data from studies prepared with the QUE$TOR software (IHS Inc., 2007) indicated that the booster pump station investment cost was equivalent to about 10 percent of the investment costs required for each 100 miles of pipeline length.

The sizing (diameter) for the regional oil and gas pipelines was based on the total assessed resources allocated to each economic zone. The regional pipeline sizing rule was conservative to allow for differences in the timing of discoveries, development rates, and production rates of different fields in the zone. Typically, the maximum pipeline capacity allows only 3 percent of the total assessed resource in the economic unit to be transported in a single year. If greater volumes of oil and gas resources are found and developed, then higher volume regional lines could be installed, and this installation would probably result in a slightly reduced regional pipeline tariff.

Regional gas pipelines from the economic zone to the future gas conditioning plant near Pump Station 1 are typically more than 50 miles long, and it is assumed that these pipelines would be high-pressure pipelines that could transport both gas and natural gas liquids in a dense phase (Corbett and others, 2003). The gas feeder lines from the field to the hub of the economic zone were assumed to be low-pressure lines, as these will be much shorter than the regional lines and require less capacity. Because the geologic assessment indicated that nonassociated gas accumulations are expected to be relatively lean, in terms of entrained liquids, it was assumed that the feeder lines transported both gas and minor amounts of NGL to the high-pressure regional pipelines. The procedures for computing the tariffs for the regional gas pipelines and the feeder lines from the outlying fields were similar to the procedures used to calculate tariffs for the crude oil pipeline.

Annual operating costs for both oil and gas pipelines were estimated to be 2 percent of the initial pipeline investment including any additional booster pumping stations. Tariffs were estimated to recover operating costs, property taxes, State and Federal income taxes, recovery of original investment, and an after-tax rate of return of 12 percent.

Table A3-1 shows the feeder and regional pipeline specifications assumed for each of the economic zones. The economic zones shown in table A3-1 correspond to the economic zones in text figure 4. The western North Slope was considered a single zone. Gas would be shipped east to the commercial gas pipeline.[21] The NPRA is divided into eight economic zones. Geologists posited that oil accumulations were more likely to occur in the northern and eastern areas of the NPRA and that the southern and western areas would be more prospective for natural gas accumulations. The volume of oil assessed in the southernmost economic zones labeled N320 and N330 is so small that a regional oil pipeline was not considered.

---

[20]Waterflood is used in pressure maintenance and to force oil to the production well in oil accumulations. In the North Slope, seawater has been used for this purpose. Nearly all of the assessed undiscovered oil accumulations were in plays located in the northern part of the North Slope, reasonably close to the coast.

[21]The assessed oil is small and, if found, could probably be shipped to the port area where the Red Dog mine concentrate is shipped, some 200 miles from the western North Slope subarea.

Table A3–1. Hypothetical pipeline system configuration distances and regional pipeline capacity by economic zone as identified in text figure 4.

[MMBO/D, millions of barrels of oil per day; BCF/D, billions of cubic feet of gas per day]

Economic zone	Commodity	Length of feeder pipeline (miles)	Length of regional pipeline (miles)	Regional pipeline capacity (MMBO/D or BCF/D)
1002 Area of the Arctic National Wildlife Refuge				
A110	oil	12	89	0.50
	gas	12	89	0.40
A120	oil	16	0	0.25
	gas	16	187	0.15
Central North Slope				
C110	oil	9	(^{1})	(^{1})
	gas	25	(^{1})	(^{1})
C120	oil	15	35	0.18
	gas	15	59	1.00
C130	oil	80	(^{1})	(^{1})
	gas	20	136	1.00
National Petroleum Reserve in Alaska				
N110	oil	10	96	0.25
	gas	10	102	0.50
N120	oil	8	167	0.25
	gas	8	170	0.75
N130	oil	17	235	0.25
	gas	17	236	1.00
N210	oil	12.5	107	0.09
	gas	12.5	114	1.00
N220	oil	17.5	173	0.06
	gas	17.5	174	1.00
N230	oil	17.5	266	0.03
	gas	17.5	268	1.00
N320	oil	200	(^{1})	(^{1})
	gas	5	218	0.14
N330	oil	300	0	0.00
	gas	17.5	282	0.42
Western North Slope				
W110	oil	200	(^{1})	(^{1})
	gas	20	340	0.75

^{1} Because of small oil volumes, only feeder lines were hypothesized for transportation to a transshipment point, either Pump Station 1 of the Trans-Alaska Pipeline System or the planned gas conditioning plant.

For the central North Slope, the northernmost economic zone (C110) would need only oil or gas feeder lines because of proximity to Pump Station 1 and the proposed natural gas conditioning plant. For the central North Slope, the southernmost economic zone (C130) was assessed to be gas prone, and so no regional oil pipeline was assumed. Future oil discoveries in the middle economic zone (C120) of the central North Slope were assumed to tie into TAPS at a location south of Pump Station 2 (text fig. 4).

The 1002 Area is considered environmentally sensitive and is very compact geographically. Because of a need to minimize the development footprint and because of the 1002 Area's compactness, the oil and gas processing facilities would be located outside the sensitive area. It is assumed that one leg of the regional pipeline would transport the produced fluids to the processing facilities in State or Native lands outside of the 1002 Federal lands. The other leg would transport the processed crude oil and gas to Pump Station 1 or the proposed gas conditioning plant (see fig. A3-1).

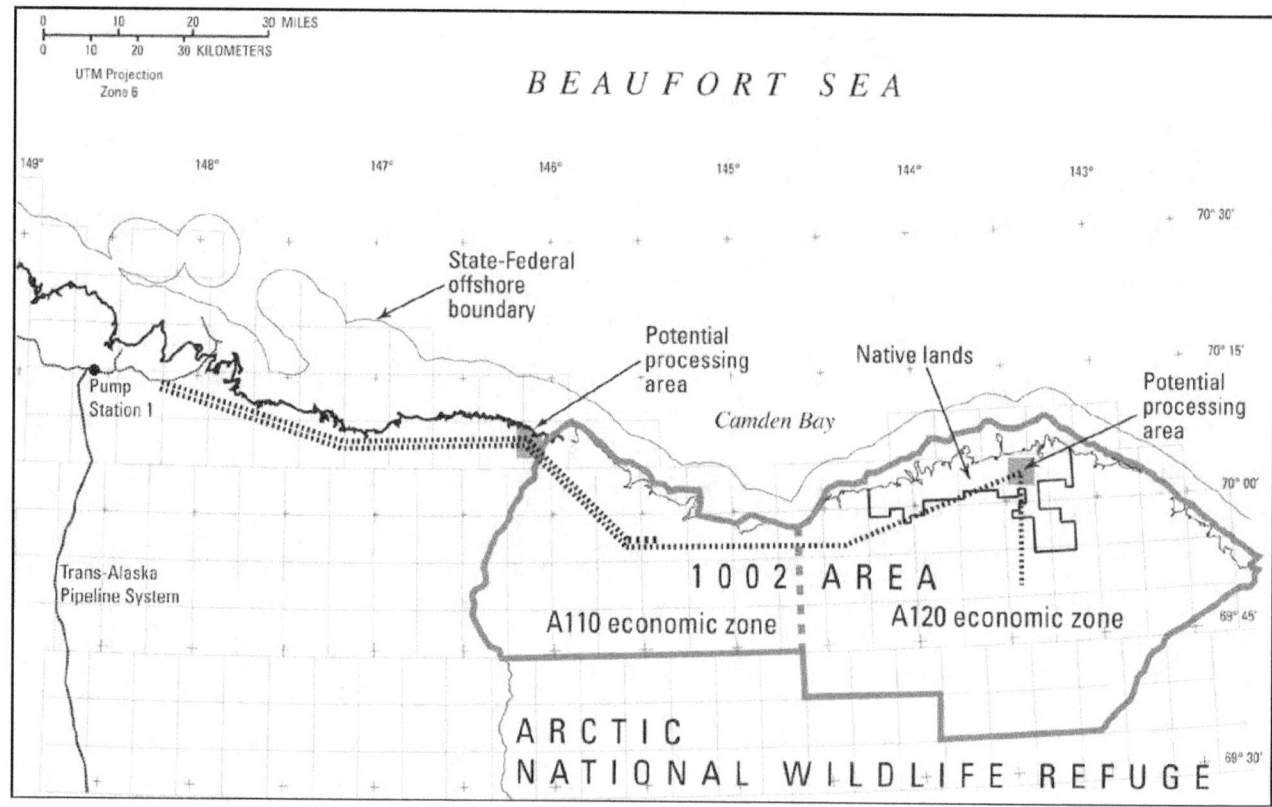

Figure A3–1. Map showing the partition of the 1002 Area of the Arctic National Wildlife Refuge into economic zones (A110 and A120) and a hypothetical, generalized regional pipeline transport system from Federal portions of the zones to processing facility areas and then to Pump Station 1 near Prudhoe Bay. The central processing areas are shaded gray. The placement of pipelines shown in the figure is for purposes of cost analysis in this study and does not imply a suggested route for the actual system (Attanasi, 2005b).

Field Development Costs

Field development costs include well drilling and completion costs and the cost of facilities. The development cost estimates are generalized because actual field development costs will depend on site-specific characteristics of prospects that are undefined today. In the process of developing generic cost functions, a number of simplifying assumptions were made to keep the economic analysis manageable. The simulated accumulations were first grouped into field size categories and into 5,000-foot subsurface depth intervals. The analysis also included the costs of vertical delineation wells for each accumulation evaluated. Development costs were estimated for a representative accumulation for each size and depth class and tested against an economic screen to determine whether the accumulations in the size and depth category were commercially developable.

Oil Field Design

Oil accumulation size (*szo*) was computed from the simulated reservoir attributes and reported in millions of barrels (MMBO):

$$szo = 7.758(t)(hps)(f)(rf_o)(ac)/(fvf_o) \text{ where } hps = p(1-S_w)$$

where for each field simulated, the reservoir attribute values are (1) net reservoir thickness, *t*, in feet, (2) porosity, *p*, as a decimal fraction, (3) hydrocarbon pore space, *hps*, as a function of *p* and S_w, where S_w is water saturation as a decimal fraction, (4) trapfill, *f*, as decimal fraction, (5) oil recovery factor, rf_o, as a decimal fraction, (6) area of closure (*ac*) in thousands of acres, and (7) the oil formation volume factor, fvf_o. The assessors provided estimates of the recovery factor (fraction of the in-place resources recoverable with the assumed technology), which is denoted rf_o. The oil formation volume factor, fvf_o, was calculated as a function of reservoir depth (Schuenemeyer, 1999, 2005). For each size and depth category, an average accumulation size was computed and used as the representative field size.

Vertical wells were assumed to have drainage areas of 160 acres (Young and Hauser, 1986). Development well productivity for oil (*wp_o*) per producing well for a given individual accumulation was calculated by the following formula:

$$wp_o = 7.758(t)(hps)(f)(rf_o)(0.16)/(fvf_o)$$

The average well recoveries were calculated on the basis of the simulated play data. The average well productivity was classified by size class of the associated simulated accumulation. Within a given play, the average well productivity tends to increase as accumulation size increases. The commonality of plays across the central North Slope and the NPRA permitted the use of average well productivity measures between subareas. The well productivity data are shown in table A3-2. Table A3-2, which is based on the play simulations, shows that oil wells for the 1002 Area are expected to be substantially more productive than oil wells elsewhere. This difference can be traced to the substantial differences in the pay thickness attribute assessed by the geologist. On the original play forms, the median pay thickness for the leading oil play (Topset) in the 1002 Area was three times that of the leading oil play (Beaufortian Upper Jurassic Topset NE) in the NPRA (see Schuenemeyer, 1999, 2003). At the 5th fractile, the leading 1002 oil play has a pay thickness of over five times that of the leading oil play in the NPRA.

The required number of production wells for the representative accumulation was calculated by dividing the recoverable accumulation volume of oil by the estimated well productivity. For conventional wells, each set of 10 producing wells required 4 injection wells (National Petroleum Council, 1981a; Young and Hauser, 1986).

Table A3–2. Estimated recovery per production well, in millions of barrels of oil (MMBO), for oil accumulations by economic zone within study subarea as identified in text figure 4.

[NPRA, National Petroleum Reserve in Alaska; CNS, central North Slope; ANWR, Arctic National Wildlife Refuge; shallow <10,000 feet; deep >10,000 feet]

Discovery size class (MMBO)	NPRA		CNS		1002 Area of ANWR			
	N110 (MMBO)	Outside N110 (MMBO)	C110 (MMBO)	Outside C110 (MMBO)	A110 shallow (MMBO)	A110 deep (MMBO)	A120 shallow (MMBO)	A120 deep (MMBO)
20–32	1.6	1.1	1.6	1.1	3.4	2.1	2.9	1.7
32–64	2.1	1.3	2.1	1.3	5.0	2.8	4.2	2.2
64–128	2.7	1.6	2.7	1.6	7.6	3.7	6.4	2.6
128–256	3.2	2.0	3.2	2.0	11.1	4.9	8.8	3.1
256–512	3.3	2.4	3.3	2.4	13.9	6.3	10.8	3.2
512–1,024	3.8	3.0	3.8	3.0	16.6	7.7	13.6	3.4
1,024–2,048	4.4	4.4	4.4	4.4	23.2	11.7	19.7	4.7
2,048–4,096	5.0	5.0	5.0	5.0	30.0	19.1	21.8	6.1

Application of horizontal well technology is attractive because it can reduce the number of production wells required to drain a pool and reduce the number of drilling pads and their sizes. It also tends to increase the proportion of the in-place oil that is recoverable and to increase the flow rates from individual wells. The drainage area and, thus, well productivity assigned to a horizontal production well depend on the natural drainage area of vertical wells and the length of the horizontal section of the well bore that is in contact with the formation. If a vertical well has a circular drainage area of 160 acres, then a horizontal well having a horizontal section of 3,000 feet would theoretically increase the drainage area to 365 acres (Joshi, 1991a,b).[22] Each producing horizontal oil well is assumed to require a horizontal injection well. This is the case in the Alpine field (Redman, 2002) near the NPRA. This reconnaissance analysis cannot capture all the trade-offs in applying horizontal technologies, such as an increase in recoverable in-place oil and a reduction in pad costs, and so the cost estimates presented here may be higher than costs based on an analysis using site data.

Gas Field Design

Gas accumulation volume (*szg*) was computed with the simulated reservoir attributes and reported in billions of cubic feet (BCF):

$$szg = 4.356(t)(hps)(f)(rf_g)(ac)(fvf_g)*10^{-8}, \text{ where } hps = p(1-S_W)$$

where for each field simulated, the reservoir attribute values are (1) net reservoir thickness, t, in feet, (2) porosity, p, as a decimal fraction, (3) hydrocarbon pore space, *hps*, as a function of p and S_W, where S_W is water saturation as a decimal fraction, (4) trapfill, f, as a decimal fraction, (5) gas recovery factor, rf_g, as a decimal fraction, (6) area of closure (*ac*) in thousands of acres, and (7) the gas formation volume factor, fvf_g. The assessors provided estimates of the recovery factor (fraction of the in-place resource that is recoverable with the assumed technology), which is denoted rf_g. The gas formation volume

---

[22]If a vertical well drains 160 acres, its expected drainage radius is 1,489 feet. The horizontal extension of the well of 3,000 feet adds 205 acres, (3,000 ft x 2 x 1,489 ft)/(43,250 ft²/acre), to the original 160-acre drainage area. This method of computing the drainage area follows Joshi (1991a). It assumes that the vertical permeability is at least equal to the horizontal permeability.

factor, *fvf*$_g$, was calculated as a function of reservoir depth. For each size and depth category, the size of the representative discovery was the average of the discoveries in that category.

A 1981 National Petroleum Council study (1981a, 1981b) on Arctic oil and gas development based its representative field designs on the assumption that the typical gas well drainage area would be 1 square mile (640 acres). Development well productivity for gas (*wp*$_g$), in billions of cubic feet per producing well, for an individual accumulation was calculated as:

$$wp_g = 4.356(t)(hps)(f)(rf_g)(0.640)(fvf_g) * 10^{-8}$$

Each gas well recovery shown in table A3-3 was computed as a volume weighted average of the computed well recoveries derived from the play reservoir attribute simulations for the NPRA and the central North Slope. Nonassociated gas has not been produced for export on the North Slope, and so there are no reliable data to predict the gas well performance. The required number of production wells for the representative accumulation was calculated by dividing the recoverable accumulation volume of gas by the estimated gas well productivity. Gas accumulations do not require water injection wells. Horizontal drilling was not applied to gas field development.

Table A3-3. Estimated recovery per production well, in billions of cubic feet of gas (BCF), for gas accumulations in any economic zone.

Discovery size class (BCF)	Recovery per well (BCF)
250–384	24.2
384–768	32.3
768–1,536	42.2
1,536–3,072	51.8
3,072–6,144	63.5
6,144–12,288	82.3
12,288–24,576	124.0

Drilling Costs

Total development well costs are computed as the product of the number of wells required for field delineation and development and of the sum of drilling, completion, and nondrilling well costs. Development well drilling and completion cost data were compiled from several sources, including industry reports (Gingrich and others, 2001; Redman, 2002; National Petroleum Council, 2003) and historical costs for Alaska oil wells reported in the Joint Association Survey (American Petroleum Institute, 1997-2005).[23] Costs were estimated for representative wells within the following vertical intervals: as much as 5,000 feet, from 5,000 feet to 10,000 feet, from 10,000 feet to 15,000 feet, and greater than 15,000 feet.

The following example illustrates the cost estimation procedure for horizontal wells. Production wells at North Slope fields are typically drilled from gravel pads that accommodate as many as 40 well collars spaced at 10-foot intervals along with production equipment. Most conventional production wells are deviated or drilled directionally to reach target locations that are horizontally offset from the drilling pad. It is assumed that the directional component adds an average of 30 percent to measured

---

[23]In some years, the number of wells drilled in Alaska far exceeded the number of wells reported in the Joint Association Survey. Further, data appear to be presented in vertical depth intervals, whereas most North Slope production wells have a significant directional component, and so actual footage drilled is greater than vertical depth.

depth for drilling that is beyond the vertical depth for wells drilled with true vertical depths to 10,000 feet. For target vertical depths of 10,000 feet and greater, the directional component requires an additional 20 percent of the vertical depth to reach target depth. At the target depth, a lateral extension of 3,000 feet is drilled and completed as a horizontal extension. If the average per-foot drilling and completion cost of $600 is assumed to be typical for the more accessible central North Slope areas, then the following equation is used to estimate horizontal development well drilling and completion costs for targets at a vertical depth of 10,000 feet (James Craig, Minerals Management Service, written communication, 2005):

$$(10,000 \text{ ft} \times 1.2 \times \$600/\text{ft}) + (3,000 \text{ ft} \times \$600/\text{ft}) = \$9.0 \text{ million per well}$$

In this example, the horizontal well adds 25 percent to the costs of drilling and completing a conventional development well, but the horizontal wells reduce the required number of producing wells by more than half, that is, productivity per producing well is more than doubled. Because each horizontal well is assumed to have one horizontal injector and the conventional well is assumed to require only 4 injection wells per set of 10 producers, the overall drilling investment per barrel recovered in the example for horizontal wells is about 89 percent of the per-barrel drilling cost compared to the standard well investment. To compensate for extra costs associated with drilling wells extending beyond 15,000 feet, it is assumed that costs increase 1 percent for each 500-foot increment in measured depth beyond 15,000 feet (James Craig, Minerals Management Service, written communication, 2008).

Estimated costs, in 2007 dollars, by 5,000-foot depth interval for conventional wells in the accessible central North Slope area are $3.9 million (with vertical depth 5,000 ft), $5.9 million (7,500 ft), $9.0 million (12,500 ft), and $14.0 million (17,500 ft). Estimated costs of corresponding horizontal wells with 3,000-ft lateral extensions in 2007 dollars are $5.9 million, $7.7 million, $11.4 million, and $17.0 million. These estimates represent average costs for drilling programs in the northern economic zone of the central North Slope (core area). Drilling costs are expected to be higher than the average for early drilling operations and lower than the average for later drilling operations in each project. Estimates of drilling costs for wells outside of the core area were increased to account for a lack of infrastructure.

Facilities Costs—Oil and Gas Development

Production facilities include drilling pads, flow lines from drilling sites, the central processing unit, and infrastructure required for housing workers, including amenities. Facilities design and cost estimates are scaled to peak production rates and field size. As of the beginning of 2004, there were eight stand-alone fields operating in northern Alaska. These fields are Prudhoe Bay, Kuparuk River, Lisburne, Milne Point, Endicott, Badami, Northstar, and Alpine. The Liberty field, formerly Tern Island, was in the final planning stages for commercial development.

There is little detailed information in the public domain about costs of facilities. An exception is a version of the Northstar development plan, including development cost estimates, that was submitted by British Petroleum Exploration (1996) to the State of Alaska for evaluation with its request for relief of profit-sharing provisions of the State lease. The Minerals Management Service (MMS) published the Liberty environmental impact statement (EIS) (Craig, 2002). A step function cost relationship that specified investment cost per barrel as a function of field size for the central North Slope was calibrated from published data and data obtained with the QUE$TOR software (IHS Inc., 2007). Table A3-4 shows estimates of oil facilities investment costs by accumulation size class assumed for the C110 economic zone of the central North Slope (text fig. 4). Facility cost estimates were increased for remote areas.

Table A3–4. Estimates of oil field facilities investment costs per barrel of oil recovered by accumulation discovery size class for facilities located in the northernmost economic zone, C110, of the central North Slope.

[MMBO, millions of barrels of oil; $/bbl, 2007 dollars per barrel of oil]

Discovery size class (MMBO)	Cost ($/bbl)
20–32	5.01
32–64	3.39
64–128	2.81
128–256	1.97
256–512	1.73
512–1,024	1.13
1,024–2,048	1.04
2,048–4,096	0.89

Since the mid-1980s, a number of newly discovered accumulations were developed as satellite units, where production fluids are processed at a nearby facility serving a larger field. The Point McIntyre and Niakuk accumulations share the central processing facilities at the Lisburne field. Prudhoe Bay production includes the following satellites: Midnight Sun, Aurora, Polaris, Borealis, and Orion. Kuparuk River production includes the following satellites: Tobasco, Tarn, Meltwater, and Palm. Thus far, nearly all of the satellite and parent fields have common ownership. The cost reduction from facility sharing depends on a number of factors, namely the composition of fluids, processing capacity of the central facility, and the relative bargaining strengths of the satellite owner and the central processing facilities owner.

Recent examples demonstrate the relationships between main field facilities and satellite development opportunities. The central processing facility at the North Slope Alpine field currently processes the produced fluid mixtures (oil, gas, and water) of wells belonging to several satellite fields located up to 25 miles away (Nelson, 2004). For gas production, the Snohvit field in the Barents Sea utilizes an 88-mile multiphase pipeline from the field to an onshore processing facility. Elsewhere in the world in deepwater offshore areas, small accumulations, even under different ownership, are produced using subsea well completion technology, and their production fluids are processed at a common production platform or facility many miles away. The advances in multiphase flow pipeline management and measurement of produced fluids have enabled these cluster and satellite production systems to monitor production in different environments and under a variety of ownership situations (Atkinson and others, 2005). Consequently, it is likely that additional cluster developments and satellite field development strategies could be used to develop new marginally sized fields on the North Slope. Under some conditions, this practice will reduce the threshold size for commercial development.

The text discusses hypothetical operations in the 1002 Area, for which the main processing facilities would be located outside the sensitive 1002 Area on either State or Native lands. In the northernmost economic zone (C110) of the central North Slope and in the northeast economic zone (N110) of the NPRA, discoveries of 130 million barrels or smaller are assumed to be developed as satellite fields. The procedure for accounting for facility-sharing charges follows an arrangement whereby it was assumed that facilities sharing would, on average, result in a 50 percent reduction in the initial facility investment cost for the satellite owner. The annual operating cost paid by the satellite owner is the sum of the annual operating cost per barrel that would be incurred if the satellite were developed as a stand-alone field plus the undiscounted per-barrel investment cost that was saved originally. Although the charges to the satellite owner resulting from this scheme could be in excess of the marginal costs incurred by the central processing facility operator, this scheme still reduces the minimum or threshold price at which a satellite becomes commercially developable while reducing risk as well.

Gas field facilities include pads, in-field pipelines, and other infrastructure. For gas discoveries, processing equipment costs are typically a smaller proportion of the total development investment because fluid handling and processing equipment is much less elaborate. Equipment could include gas dehydration and removal of other components but not an NGL plant because natural gas liquids are delivered through the gas pipelines to the zone hub. Table A3-5 shows the unit investment cost estimates by gas field size class for the economic zone C110 of the central North Slope. Facilities investment costs were increased for remote areas.

Table A3-5. Estimates of gas field facilities investment costs per thousand cubic feet of gas recovered by accumulation size class for facilities located in the northernmost economic zone, C110, of the central North Slope.

[BCF, billion cubic feet of gas; $/MCF, 2007 dollars per thousand cubic feet]

Discovery size class (BCF)	Cost ($/MCF)
250–384	0.64
384–768	0.37
768–1,536	0.32
1,536–3,072	0.26
3,072–6,144	0.24
6,144–12,288	0.20
12,288–24,576	0.20

Production Profile

Oil Discoveries

Future discoveries are assumed to attain peak annual rates of production equal to a percentage of the accumulation's ultimate oil recovery. Table A3-6 lists the assumptions relating to the representative oil accumulation production profiles. An accumulation with less than 512 million barrels of recoverable oil is assumed to reach peak production in the year production starts. For accumulations with more than 512 million barrels, peak production occurs in the second production year. Peak production is maintained for several years; thereafter, annual production declines 12 percent per year.

At first glance, the 12 percent field production decline rate appears unduly steep. Observed field decline rates are typically more subdued because of the application of enhanced recovery techniques to prolong field life. However, the appropriate enhanced recovery application and its success often depend on site-specific conditions. Costs and production streams for oil discoveries calculated in this analysis include primary recovery and the application of waterflood.

The volume of produced water was projected by using typical field production profiles for oil, the degree of field depletion, and the water-cut functions presented by Thomas and others (1991). Figure A3-2 shows the percentage of water expected in oil production with depletion of the field with a Kuparuk-type production and figure A3-3 shows the production characteristics for an Alpine-type field. Produced volumes of natural gas and natural gas liquids were projected by using annual oil production, the expected values of the gas-to-oil ratio, and NGL-to-gas ratios associated with the representative field's size and depth classification.

Table A3–6. Oil discovery production profiles used in the economic analysis.

[MMBO, millions of barrels of oil]

Discovery size class (MMBO)	Year reaches peak	Peak as percent of recoverable	Years of peak production
20–32	1	11.00	3
32–64	1	11.00	3
64–128	1	11.00	3
128–256	1	10.00	3
256–512	1	10.00	3
512–1,024	2	9.00	3
1,024–2,048	2	6.75	4
2,048–4,096	2	6.50	7

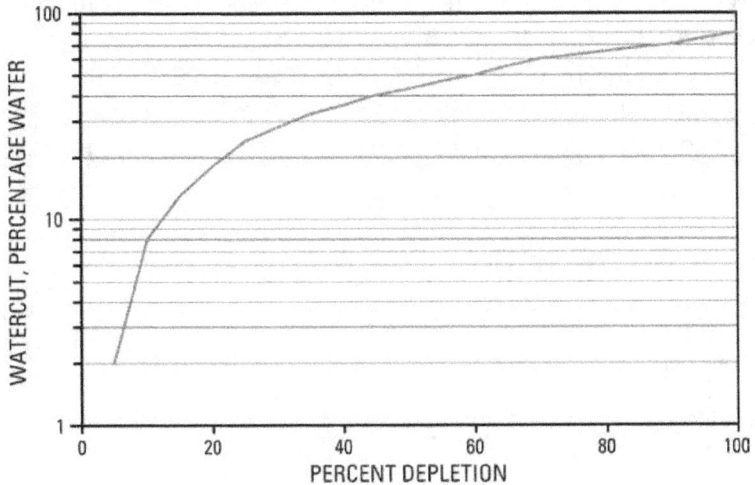

Figure A3–2. Graph showing percentage of water in oil production stream as a function of reservoir depletion for Kuparuk-type reservoirs; data are from Thomas and others (1991).

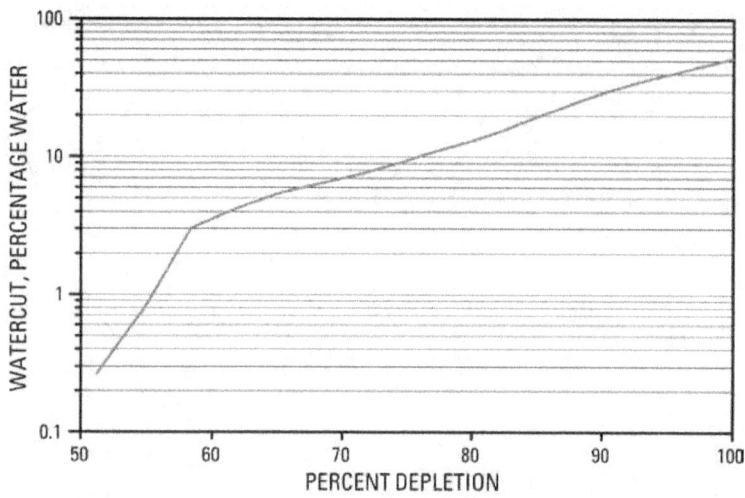

Figure A3–3. Graph showing percentage of water in oil production stream as a function of reservoir depletion for the Alpine-type reservoirs in the National Petroleum Reserve in Alaska; data are from ARCO Alaska Inc. and others (1998).

Gas Discoveries

Representative gas field production profiles were developed using data from the production history of accumulations of similar sizes in other areas. In particular, the production histories of recent Gulf of Mexico fields were analyzed to determine the relationship between peak field production and their known recoverable gas partitioned into field size categories. With these peak production rates as a function of estimated field size, it was assumed that field production would be held constant until 75 to 80 percent of the field's original reserves is produced. The period of constant production is then followed by a rapid decline at a rate of 24 percent per year. These production profiles were used as an analog for the North Slope gas production profiles. Table A3-7 lists the gas production parameters assumed for this study.

Table A3–7. Gas discovery production profiles used in the economic analysis.

[BCF, billion cubic feet of gas]

Discovery size class (BCF)	Year reaches peak	Peak as percent of recoverable	Years of peak production
250–384	1	7.00	12
384–768	2	6.50	13
768–1,536	2	6.50	13
1,536–3,072	2	6.50	13
3,072–6,144	3	6.50	14
6,144–12,288	3	6.00	14
12,288–24,576	3	6.00	14

Operating Costs

Annual operating costs include labor, supervision, overhead and administration, communications, catering, supplies, consumables, well service and workovers, facilities maintenance and insurance, and transportation. Some of these costs, such as well workover and labor costs, have declined dramatically during the last decade owing to the introduction of coiled tubing technology and the introduction of automation in field operations. However, the cost declines related to technology innovations have been partially offset by recent labor and materials cost increases.

Oil Fields

Annual operating costs, on a per-barrel-of-crude-oil basis, were estimated as a function of fluid volumes and number of operating wells (Craig, 2002). In particular, for the central North Slope, the annual oil discovery operating cost is estimated to be the sum of $2 per barrel of annual fluid flow and $2 million per production well per year. The produced fluids, consisting primarily of oil and water volumes, were projected annually using field production forecasts and water-cut functions (see figs. A3-2 and A3-3) from Thomas and others (1991) and ARCO Alaska Inc. and others (1998), so that per-barrel costs of produced oil increased as the water cut increased and the field approached depletion. Water production is initially very small. Operating cost estimates were cross checked with estimates from the initial year cost predictions from the QUE$TOR software (IHS Inc., 2007).

Gas Fields

There are no commercially operating gas discoveries that export natural gas outside the North Slope, and so estimates of operating costs relied on data from studies based on the QUE$TOR software (IHS Inc., 2007). The estimates for operating costs for gas discoveries for the central North Slope are presented in table A3-8.

Table A3–8. Gas field unit production cost used in the economic analysis.

[BCF, billions of cubic feet of gas; $/MCF, 2007 dollars per thousand cubic feet]

Discovery size class (BCF)	Cost ($/MCF)
250–384	1.75
384–768	1.38
768–1,536	0.80
1,536–3,072	0.50
3,072–6,144	0.37
6,144–12,288	0.26

Appendix 4. Federal and Alaska Taxes

Royalties

Royalties are payments to the resource owner. The assessment area included areas where mineral rights were owned by the Federal Government, the Alaska State Government, and Native corporations. Actual royalty rates for State and Native lands can vary substantially for different parcels and periods depending on the economic conditions in the oil and gas industry. To simplify the analysis, it was assumed that each oil or gas project bore the 12.5 percent royalty payment of the gross value received at the wellhead to the owner of the mineral rights. This cost was modeled by assuming that royalty was paid in kind to the owner.

Alaska State Taxes

Alaska's Clear and Equitable Share Tax

The Alaska Clear and Equitable Share (ACES) tax replaced the Petroleum Production Tax (PPT) in 2007. The PPT had previously replaced the State severance tax in 2006. The ACES and PTT taxes are on the net income of the producer. Because the ACES tax is calculated from a corporate accounting stance, certain simplifications were needed to apply it to project analysis. The tax applies to oil, gas, and natural gas liquids. The tax rates are expressed in terms of barrels of oil equivalent, and so these commodities were converted to barrels of oil equivalent. The tax described here is specific to North Slope producers.

Procedure

The tax liability is calculated on the basis of petroleum production value (PVT) that is taxable and the tax rate. The taxable barrels exclude the royalty rate barrels. The corporate PVT is the product of the net wellhead price and taxable barrels (barrels net of royalty) minus operating costs (including property taxes) and capital expenditures taken that year. If the PVT is not positive, the tax liability is 4 percent of the product of the wellhead price and taxable barrels.

The tax rate escalates with increases in the PVT per barrel. When the PVT is positive but does not exceed $30 per barrel, the tax rate is 25 percent. From $30 per barrel to $92.50 per barrel, the tax rate increases 0.4 percent per dollar for each dollar the PVT is greater than $30 per barrel. At a PVT of $92.50 per barrel, the tax rate is 50 percent. The tax rate increases to a maximum rate of 75 percent from 50 percent in steps of 0.1 percent per dollar for each dollar the PVT is greater than $92.50.

The tax liability is the product of the tax rate and the PVT for the company. Once the tax liability is computed, tax credits can offset part of the taxes owed. If previous years had negative PVTs, then 25 percent of those losses can be carried forward to later years as a tax credit. The qualified capital expenditures (QCE) tax credit amounts to 20 percent of the capital expenditures. The accounting calculation for the tax rate, tax liability, and credits is done on a corporate basis. Tax credits may be monetized by being sold to other North Slope operators. It should be noted that not only do corporate-wide North Slope capital expenditures reduce the current year's tax rate by reducing the PVT per barrel but also that the 20 percent QCE credit reduces the actual net tax liability (Greg Bidwell, Alaska Department of Natural Resources, written communication, 2008).

This analysis applied the following simplified version of the tax to the project level. During production, the PVT, tax rates, and tax liability were computed for the single project. Initial capital for expenditures for field delineation and development prior to production were totaled. Twenty percent of this total became a tax credit against future ACES tax liability. In addition, 25 percent of the annual losses incurred before the start of production were carried forward as a tax credit to offset ACES tax liability. It was assumed that 10 percent of the annual operating costs were expenditures that qualified as capital expenditures (well workover and some replacement machinery).

Ad Valorem Tax

Alaska's ad valorem tax is 2 percent of the economic value of pipelines, facilities, and equipment. For pipelines, a 20-year life was assumed. For tangible well costs, oil field equipment costs, and facilities costs, depreciation of the asset was based on the unit of production method.[24]

State Income Tax

For planning purposes, the Alaska State agencies use 2 to 4 percent of net income. The rate used here was 4 percent of net income. Depreciation of capital assets associated with oil field development is permitted on a unit-of-production basis. For other capital, depreciation depends on the economic life of the equipment.

State Conservation Tax

The State conservation surcharge tax was assumed to be set at $0.05 per barrel of oil.

Federal Income Taxes

A Federal income tax rate of 35 percent of taxable income was assumed. According to the 1986 Tax Reform Act, 30 percent of development well drilling costs is classified as tangible cost and therefore capitalized over 7 years. Of the remaining 70 percent of drilling cost (that is, the intangible drilling costs), 30 percent is depreciated over 5 years and the remaining 70 percent is expensed immediately.

---

[24]As a practical matter, as long as the asset is operating, the basis for the tax will not be smaller than 25 percent of either the initial investment or the asset's estimated replacement value (Greg Bidwell, written communication, 2008).

www.ingramcontent.com/pod-product-compliance
Lightning Source LLC
Chambersburg PA
CBHW080438290526
45791CB00008BA/2545